ECONOMIC THOUGHT:
A BRIEF HISTORY

ECONOMIC THOUGHT

A BRIEF HISTORY

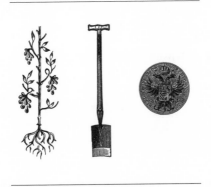

HEINZ D. KURZ
TRANSLATED BY JEREMIAH RIEMER

COLUMBIA UNIVERSITY PRESS
NEW YORK

Columbia University Press
Publishers Since 1893
New York   Chichester, West Sussex
Copyright © Verlag C. H. Beck oHG 2013
Translation copyright © Columbia University Press 2016
All rights reserved

Library of Congress Cataloging-in-Publication Data
Names: Kurz, Heinz D., author.
Title: Economic thought : a brief history / Heinz D. Kurz ; translated by
   Jeremiah Riemer.
Other titles: Geschichte des ökonomischen Denkens. English
Description: New York : Columbia University Press, 2016. | Includes
   bibliographical references and index.
Identifiers: LCCN 2015038035 | ISBN 9780231172585 (cloth : alk. paper) |
   ISBN 9780231540759 (e-book)
Subjects: LCSH: Economics—History.
Classification: LCC HB75 .K85713 2016 | DDC 330.15—dc23
LC record available at http://lccn.loc.gov/2015038035

COVER DESIGN: Jordan Wannemacher

CONTENTS

PREFACE

This book is a translation of a revised and somewhat enlarged version of my *Geschichte des ökonomischen Denkens* published in 2013 by C.H. Beck in Munich. The German version appeared in the series Wissen (Knowledge), which introduces readers to basically all fields of knowledge—the sciences, humanities, history, the arts, religions, and so on. Each paperback typically comprises 128 pages and is directed at all readers interested in its subject, no prior knowledge needed.

This also applies to the present book. It has been written in a nontechnical style that seeks to ease entry into the fascinating world of economics. All you need is to be able to read and to think. While there are a few diagrams, some simple numerical examples, and occasionally symbols to represent certain economic magnitudes, the reader should easily be able to master them. To paraphrase Albert Einstein: To read this book you need not be possessed of special talents. It suffices that you are passionately curious. Given the overwhelming importance of the economic sphere in the world in which we live, who could afford not to be passionately curious about what economists have to say about it?

The present text is somewhat longer than the original German one and is directed at a more international, especially an American, readership. Contributions to economics coming from the "New World" are now dealt with in much greater detail at the cost of topics that are of special interest to the German-speaking reader only.

In the course of working on the German and the American version I received most valuable comments and suggestions from many friends and colleagues. I am especially grateful to Manfred Holler, Kenji Mori, Heinz Rieter, Hans-Peter Spahn, and Erich Streissler. Thanks go also to Gilbert Faccarello, Duncan Foley, the late Pierangelo Garegnani, Christian Gehrke, Harald Hagemann, Geoff Harcourt, Peter Kalmbach, Stan Metcalfe, Edward J. Nell, Neri Salvadori, the late Paul A. Samuelson, Bertram Schefold, Richard Sturn, Ian Steedman, and Hans-Michael Trautwein for multiple discussions over many years of the matters involved. I should also like to thank an anonymous reviewer of the American text for useful advice. Special thanks go to Jonathan Beck, my editor at C.H. Beck; Bridget Flannery-McCoy, my editor at Columbia University Press; and Jeremiah Riemer, the translator. The collaboration with Bridget and Jeremiah was effective and pleasant, and if the argument should by now be easy to follow and a reasonably good read it is to no small degree because of them.

It is now up to the "passionately curious" readers—the object of desire of all authors—to form a judgment on the outcome of all the effort and endeavor that went into this book.

Graz, June 8, 2015
Heinz D. Kurz

We continually meet with old friends in new dresses.
—ALFRED MARSHALL

Old friends come disguised to the party.
—JOSEPH A. SCHUMPETER

The ideas of economists and political philosophers, both when they are right and when they are wrong, are more powerful than is commonly understood. Indeed the world is ruled by little else.
—JOHN MAYNARD KEYNES

ECONOMIC THOUGHT:
A BRIEF HISTORY

INTRODUCTION

A history of economic thought in some 200 pages? Impossible! Or maybe not?

In 1914 Joseph A. Schumpeter (1883–1950) published his "Economic Doctrine and Method: A Historical Sketch," a hundred-page essay tracing an arc from antiquity to what was then modern times. If Schumpeter's one hundred pages suffice to treat the subject matter up to the beginning of the twentieth century, 220 pages should certainly be enough to include developments up to the century's end. That much space really is sufficient—assuming we acknowledge taking the risk of leaving some gaps in our coverage.

Would it suffice to take Schumpeter's old text and simply append an ample supplement of some 200 pages? Unfortunately not. The history of a field is not something written once and for all. It is a constantly changing construct in which new generations that have their own problems and ideas grapple with the problems and ideas of older generations. With the passage of time there is a change in what Schumpeter called the "vision" of how an economic system works, and our understanding of the old masters changes along with that vision. It is a serious misunderstanding to believe that history is something that was once upon a time but is no more: "History is not was, it is," said William Faulkner. So much the worse that this misunderstanding is widespread—both inside and outside the field of economics.

Every generation writes its own history and is keen not only on being original but on being perceived as such. But each generation also searches for meaningful progenitors so it can share in their renown and brilliance. With a new appreciation of problems, it discovers sides to the old masters that had eluded previous generations. Hence the notion of continuity and change in the field is itself an idea subjected to an everlasting process of continuity and change. Schumpeter's old essay, highly readable today, is part of history. Reading it shows how much perspectives have changed since then, which insights have been acquired and which ones lost, how research methods have changed, and a great deal more.

According to the Japanese economist Takashi Negishi (b. 1933), there is "nothing new under the sun" in economics. Everything, he contends, can be found in the classic economic texts. This is certainly an exaggeration, but it contains a kernel of truth. There are a number of ideas, long familiar, that take on new meaning when given a different form or considered in a fresh context. New knowledge in economics is made up, above all, of old particles of knowledge combined in new ways. The image of a tree of knowledge constantly sprouting new branches symbolizes the process. But some branches, already regarded as dead, suddenly begin to sprout anew.

Does this mean that economics preserves everything that is correct and valuable and disposes of everything that is wrong and misleading? Is the market for economic ideas a perfectly functioning selection mechanism? Unfortunately, the answer is no.

The formation of bubbles in financial markets is well known. Bubbles occur because people form a picture about a segment of reality, others adopt this picture, and herd behavior follows. Economists also form a picture about a segment of reality, which can sometimes sharpen but sometimes obstruct our understanding of the world. A picture can be misleading without this fact being recognized as such immediately. If such ideas are amplified via positive feedback within the scholarly enterprise by way of faculty appointments, rankings in journals, the allocation of research funds, and by honors and prizes, this results in an intrascholarly bubble. In light of the complexity of the subject, this is a major danger that cannot be reliably eliminated. But anyone acquainted with the history of economic thought, both where it triumphed and where it went astray, will be aware of this danger and will be on guard.

Finally, it is important to remember that the huge changes in the economy over the last few centuries have also changed our view of it. Take figure 1.1, adapted from a work by the American economic historian Robert W. Fogel (1926–2013). It presents the history of humankind at a glance, showing the relationship of the development of world population to important events and technological inventions. It is not until the turn of the eighteenth century that development and growth begins to accelerate, after the discovery of the New World, the Second Agricultural Revolution, and the beginning of the Industrial Revolution. Europe and its offspring abroad (the United States, Canada, Australia, and New Zealand) attain a path of

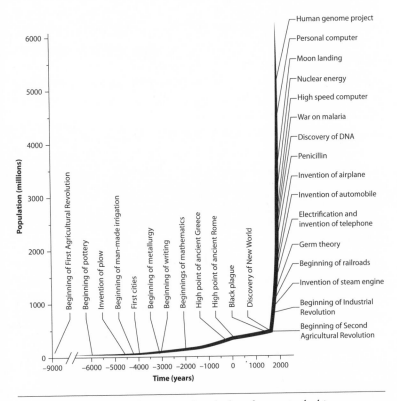

FIGURE 1.1 Population growth and selected events in the history of technology. Adapted from Robert W. Fogel, 1999, "Catching Up with the Economy." *American Economic Review*, 89(1): 1–21.

high and sustained economic growth, creating a growing wealth gap between these areas of settlement and the rest of the world—the "Great Divergence" (discussed by Kenneth Pomeranz in his book of the same name).

It is no coincidence that the study of political economy blossoms just as European economies take off, the point at which the curve bends sharply upward in the illustration. The economic dynamism that is unfolding and the forces operating within that dynamic call out to be understood and applied to economic policy. Thereafter, humankind embarks on an entirely different path, whose end we do not know.

There are different ways of approaching the history of economic thought. The focus of this volume is on economic theories: their formation, their conclusiveness and place within the field, and their applicability to economic policy. I draw attention to those economists and their teachings I regard as especially important. I can only hope that no really big fish have slipped through the mesh of the net I have cast.

Let me acknowledge, at the onset, some of the gaps in coverage. The focus is on European intellectual traditions and their continuation in the so-called Western world, but of course it is a fact that all advanced civilizations have produced notable achievements in the exploration of economic matters. The reader interested in the history of Chinese economic thought is asked to consult, for example, Hu Jichuang (2009); an overview of Islamic economic thought is provided, for example, by El-Ashker and Wilson (2006). Beyond some geographic gaps, there are also some gaps in subjects covered, such as the omission of business administration, managerial economics, and econometrics.

Finally, a remark about the literature cited is warranted: the references and bibliography draws the reader's attention to some important primary works but also to books and articles that summarize and acknowledge important economists, schools of economic theory, or the development of subdisciplines in the field. These contain all the necessary information to easily trace the primary literature in which the reader might be interested. Details mentioned in the text may be found in the works listed in the references and bibliography.

I

EARLY ECONOMIC THOUGHT

I n this chapter I summarize what the ancients, Scholastics (ca. 1100–1600), and mercantilists (ca. 1500–1800) thought about economic activity. Their observations had shared characteristics: all were still fairly unsystematic, did not encompass all fields of economic conduct, and were oriented toward prescription. These thinkers were less concerned with describing and analyzing economic activity as it was (positive economics) than with how it ideally should be (normative economics). In antiquity and Scholasticism, economic statements were actually part of moral philosophy and concerned the application of ethical principles to economic life. In mercantilism, economic investigations came up above all in the writings and pamphlets of merchant capitalists engaged in long-distance trade who were eager to pass off their particular interests as the general interest. They were keen to secure the support of the nation-state to protect their vessels and trading posts abroad, and so praised the advantages of exporting merchandise of a greater value than the value of imported merchandise—which would fill the king's coffers with the precious metals used for exchange.

A number of concepts that strike us as self-evident today, such as competition and progress, either are absent in these early writings or are only present in rudimentary fashion—reflecting the economic environment at the time. In the era of antiquity and Scholasticism, economic conditions were essentially stationary, and even for the mercantilists development and growth were rather modest and confined to a few areas.

ANTIQUITY Human beings have always made economic observations. In order to survive, we have to consume, and in order to consume, we have to produce. With the development of pictures and writing came records of economic activity. For our earliest ancestors, "producing" meant first and foremost hunting and gathering, and cave paintings in Europe that date to the Upper Paleolithic period show hunting scenes with technical and organizational knowledge embodied in weapons. Elementary economic information later became a public good for all who could read. In the heyday of Mesopotamia around 4,000 years ago, for instance, clay bricks at the gateway to Babylon were emblazoned with information about the annual grain harvest along with the expenses it entailed, also measured in grain. The difference between harvest and expenses gives us the surplus product of grain for the year in question. This surplus served to maintain the families engaged in agriculture as well as the ruler and his royal court of civil servants, the army, and so on. The size of the surplus product provides information about the welfare, economic productivity, and political and military power of the community. These clay tablets are perhaps the first national income account in human history.

GREEK ECONOMY AND ECONOMICS The Greek mode of production at the time of Plato (427–347 B.C.) and his student Aristotle (384–322 B.C.) was based on slavery and on traditions and institutions that changed very slowly, including the political constitution of the city-state. The focus of attention was on the "good life" of the full citizens—a static concept—and the regulatory and institutional framework conducive to it. Production took place in nearly autarchic households—thus coining the term "economy" from the Greek *oikos*, meaning "house," and *nomos*, meaning "law." *Oikonomia* thus means "household management" or the rules according to which a household or business is best run.

The observations of philosophers at that time revolved around questions of proper business and economic management, and the aim was to harmonize the economically useful with the morally advisable and politically reasonable. Such questions encompassed private life as well as the public economy and the financing of state business. While state financing was initially facilitated by voluntary donations, tribute payments from colonies, and services from citizens, over time there was an increase in compulsory contributions—first in the taxation of immigrant city dwellers without citizenship (metics) and finally even of citizens. Since taxation was based on wealth, the question arose as to how wealth should be ascertained—leading to a distinction between visible and invisible (or concealable) wealth. Taxes on visible wealth such as houses, fields, groves, tools, and work animals were harder to evade than taxes on invisible wealth such as money or interest payable from credit transactions. Herein, arguably, lies one of the sources of the opposition to credit and interest that permeated economic thinking in the Roman Catholic Church up until the nineteenth century (see the section on "Scholasticism" later in this chapter) and in the Islamic world up until today.

PLATO Plato, scion of an aristocratic house, saw the management of a household and of the state, the polis, as closely related. In both cases what mattered was the welfare of those entrusted to the master's care—be it master of the house or ruler of the state. This welfare had a material component that was a means to an end—the good life—and not an end in itself. In *The Republic*, Plato outlined the essential features of an ideal state—the first fully elaborated social utopia in history. Plato's focus was on realizing ethical norms, on arriving at the truly good. The pursuit of this goal demanded adherence to strict rules and the punishment of violators. (Plato's blueprint is therefore said to have totalitarian features; and since there was only common property at the top of the social pyramid, it has also been interpreted as a kind of primitive communism.)

In order for this stratified, hierarchical society to reproduce itself, said Plato, everyone must assume his appropriate place. He set the philosophers or philosopher-kings at the top of this ideal commonwealth, followed by guardians of the community, who live in an all-male brotherhood and are full-fledged citizens. A warrior caste defends the state, and their campaigns of conquest are regarded as just by Plato if they serve to defend the truly good. Below the guardians are the artisans and merchants, and the metics—nonnative citizens without rights (and their slaves). Full citizens (and their slaves) are prohibited from working in these trades. Private property is allowed here, but profit seeking is despised, because Plato conceived of wealth as a corrupter of man and saw the danger of wealth turning into power and ending in tyranny. Plato therefore advocated the redistribution of property to ward off this danger.

There is a close relationship between the social stratification Plato envisioned in *The Republic* and his understanding of the division of labor as the foundation of the commonwealth. His basic view was that a person's natural aptitudes and talents should decide his place in society. If everyone does what he is best at doing, then everything that is done will be done well. Accordingly, Plato is primarily concerned with the best possible deployment and allocation of natural talents and not (as later, in the case of Adam Smith) with the productivity-enhancing impact of the division of labor. Specialization and learning by doing, which can strengthen but also thwart naturally occurring differences in human aptitudes, Plato mentioned only in passing.

He viewed the social and professional hierarchy as static, not dynamic. According to him, the coordination of the various kinds of labor performed in society is effected in part through command and central administration (as in the military) and in part through markets.

Money, Plato insisted in *The Republic*, should serve only a single purpose: that of a means of payment. It must not be used as a means of storing value (and thus of hoarding), because accumulating wealth has no finite limit and therefore is unnatural. He despised the taking of interest as improper. He did not provide detailed thoughts about price formation and thus about the incomes of producers and merchants.

ARISTOTLE Descended from the ranks of the metics, Aristotle did not agree with his mentor Plato about everything. For instance, Aristotle advocated private property by using an argument that reappears in the work of later thinkers: people treat personal property with greater care than they do communal property. This has come to be known as the "problem of the commons."

Aristotle's observations revolved around the organization and management of the self-sufficient household economy. What are the rights and duties of the master, the father, the spouse, the children, and the slaves? The latter seem to him, in spite of some reservations on account of their status—is it ethical to treat human beings as property?—as indispensable for the good life of free citizens (and philosophers), who should be spared any concern with attending to their material well-being.

Like Plato, Aristotle distinguished between different kinds of "acquisitive arts"—the means by which households and people make a living and meet their needs and wants. Its "natural form" (*oikonomiké*) enabled the Greek citizen and his family to have a good life by producing and procuring goods. Aristotle saw the good as limited by nature, and hence this type of acquisitive art had a finite goal. One could use as a near synonym a term introduced by Herbert Simon (1916–2001), "satisficing": seeking enough of what's required to satisfy one's needs corresponding to one's position in society rather than trying to maximize one's gain.

Aristotle contrasts this natural form of acquisition with the "unnatural acquisitive art" of *chrematistics* (from *chrema*, meaning money). It serves the end of enrichment, of acquisition for acquisition's sake, which is "unnatural," because it is unlimited. Aristotle locates the origin of *chrematistics* in trade and money, which emerged to facilitate exchange. But since money can also serve as a store of value, there is a tendency to hoard treasure. The acquisition of money becomes an end in itself. As the story of King Midas shows, the man who strives for the greatest possible wealth runs the danger of dying from hunger—everything he touches turns to gold. Aristotle viewed credit transactions and interest as especially reprehensible forms of *chrematistics*. For him, every kind of interest is usury, because it "makes a gain out of money itself."

Justice is a pervasive theme of Aristotle's work, as can be seen in his observations on markets in the *Nicomachean Ethics*. One issue discussed in this text is distributive justice. Aristotle distinguishes between the "use value" of a thing and its "exchange value"; the former concerns its objective usefulness at satisfying certain needs and the latter the amount of money (or other goods) one receives in exchange for it. The producer's attention, according to *Nicomachean Ethics,* should be on the quality of the use value rather than the amount of the exchange value.

Like Plato, Aristotle did not furnish any positive analysis of how prices are formed; instead, he presented a norm that prices are supposed to obey. This norm (which refers back to the stability and reproduction of stratified Greek society) says that prices should guarantee an appropriate distribution of wealth and honor. The social status of those participating in exchange transactions should be respected and reproduced by the market. Translated into our times and using an example by Joseph Stiglitz (b. 1943): bank clerks ought to get a salary that allows them to feed and house themselves and their families and to be properly dressed at the counter. The economy is thus the accomplice of the principles on which the polis rests. The stratification of society is also reflected in Aristotle's attitude toward physical labor; performed by the lower strata of society and by slaves and scorned by the upper strata, such work lacked dignity and therefore value in his view.

The thoughts of the Greek philosophers were translated into Arabic and then also into Latin and were discussed, absorbed, and elaborated in the respective philosophical, theological, and juridical traditions. One encounters the prohibition of interest both in the Old Testament of the Bible and the Qur'an. In his *Confessions*, Augustine of Hippo (A.D. 354–430) incorporated some of Plato and Aristotle's ideas into a Christian view of the world, which left a deep imprint on the thinking in the Occident. The ideas of the Greeks found their way into Islamic economic thinking and keep exerting their influence, especially on Islamic banking.

Let me now turn to the teachings of the churchmen in Europe's Middle Ages.

SCHOLASTICISM Christian teachers continued to develop the economic views of the ancients, especially those of Aristotle, and also incorporated ideas from the Bible and from Roman law. The so-called Scholastic school's most important thinker was Thomas Aquinas (1225–1274) with his three-volume *Summa theologiae*; Francisco de Vitoria (1483–1546), and his school of Salamanca, was another notable Scholastic. Like Plato and Aristotle, Aquinas took an approach that was predominantly normative and concentrated on similar topics: the "just price," interest and usury, and just taxation ("Render to Caesar the things that are Caesar's").

However, unlike the Greek thinkers before them, the focus of the Scholastics was not on how to attain the good life in this world but how to avoid hell in the next one. The subject was man according to the Old Testament, driven out of Paradise and punished for his sins by eking out an existence full of hardship and privation. Hard work grants him survival and a life occasionally punctuated by miracles as a reward for profound demonstrations of faith. According to Scholastic economic thought, the answer to the material hardship experienced by large segments of the population was not higher production and economic growth but self-restraint and the repression of needs.

The heart of Scholasticism was the doctrine concerning usury. A core argument was that money is sterile—it cannot "breed offspring." Another argument said that since God gave time to all men equally, merely letting time elapse between taking and paying back a loan does not justify any interest. A third argument rested on a feature of the medieval economy— the absence of sustained growth—which meant that most loans were to consumers rather than producers. The duty of a Christian, argued the Scholastics, was to help those who had innocently fallen into need and not exploit them or exacerbate their condition by levying interest. *Fenus pecuniae funus est animae*—interest from money is the death of the soul. A good society demanded that its members live virtuously.

What happens, however, when trade and industry pick up in Europe, as in the twelfth and thirteenth centuries, and even more so when the economy embarks on a path of sustained economic growth, as in the wake of the Industrial Revolution, and additional liquid means are required in order to finance investments? The ancient and medieval economies, wherein interest was frowned upon, were more or less stationary and managed to reproduce themselves without major changes year in and year out (leaving aside times with particularly good or bad harvests, wars, and epidemics). As the economy embarked upon a path of sustained economic growth, economic analysis had to change to account for this. The Aristotelian and Scholastic view was gradually pushed into the background (although it did not entirely disappear from view; some of Scholasticism's ideas reappear in Austrian economics, for instance, covered in chap. 4) and after flowering in the thirteenth and fourteenth centuries, Scholasticism ended with the decline of the school of Salamanca in the sixteenth century. In the Salamanca school there were already clear pronouncements of positive economics, which assumed center stage with classical economics, the subject of chapter 2. But before dealing with the classical economists, we must first turn to what Adam Smith (1723–1790) called "mercantilism" and to what in the German-speaking world is known as "cameralism." The ideas assembled under these names do not constitute a coherent body of thought. This does not mean they were unimportant. They in fact exerted a great influence on economic policy then and still do today.

MERCANTILISM AND CAMERALISM The zenith of mercantilist thought stretched from the sixteenth to the eighteenth century and was accompanied by the creation and rise of nation-states in Europe, the discovery of new worlds, and the expansion of long-distance trade. However, mercantilist ideas and economic policies remain quite widespread. Mercantilism owes its lasting renown to the extremely critical treatment that classical economist Adam Smith gave it in *An Inquiry into the Nature and Causes of the Wealth of Nations* (1776). It was Smith who coined the term "mercantilism" to describe an amalgamation of different ideas; the name stuck, despite the fact that it was not a truly unified system of thought.

The wish to define philosophical systems, said Ludwig Wittgenstein (1889–1951), is frequently like the attempt to classify clouds by their shape; the same could be said of Smith's concept of mercantilism. To be sure, mercantilist economic thinking lacked coherence, systematic classification, and comprehensive coverage of all economic fields. Its proponents were not dispassionate scholars but rather profit-oriented businessmen and civil servants eager to fill the state's coffers. Their main concern was increasing the power of a nation by amassing new territory, protecting national commerce, forming colonies, managing the population, and—crucially—exporting more goods than were imported.

The mercantilist focus on running a trade surplus was directly connected with their conception of a nation's wealth. As English thinker Thomas Mun (1571–1641) put it in his book *England's Treasure by Forraign Trade* (written around 1630): England's wealth is increased "wherein wee . . . sell more to strangers yearly than wee consume of theirs in value." He and other mercantilists advocated export promotion (export premiums) and import restrictions (tariffs and other barriers to trade) to achieve this.

While later critics called this economic policy irrational, it was much less so than it might look at first sight. With precious metals circulating as money in the form of coins, a country facing growing markets required ever greater quantities of gold—the "good of goods," as it was widely called. If a country could not produce precious metals on its own (as in the case of England, which had no significant deposits) then a positive trade balance could bring in the needed gold. Another approach, sanctioned by the English crown, was piracy: capturing Spanish ships that were transporting gold and silver from Central and South America. Buccaneers like John Hawkins and Francis Drake were highly decorated for stealing money in service to the English crown. As tensions grew between expansionist nation-states, such wealth also became important as a preparation for future wars. There were still no large standing armies, so a properly filled state treasury was the best guarantee for mustering one quickly—"money is the sinews of war," as one observer perceptively remarked. Finally, export promotion stimulated domestic production and employment, while import restriction curbed these for foreign countries: goods produced at home gave employment to domestic workers and goods not demanded abroad had no employment effect there. Joan Robinson (1903–1983) later called this the beggar-my-neighbor policy: a country exports unemployment along with its export surplus. (Note that we find this kind of policy even in our time—take, for instance, the export surpluses enjoyed by Germany and Japan after World War II or China today as the result of undervalued domestic currencies.)

Not all mercantilist authors measured national wealth by the stock of precious metals in the treasury of the crown. To some, it was clear that economic activity is stifled when money is withdrawn from circulation and hoarded—and some (both within and without the mercantilist school) also recognized that the circulation of a growing money supply would sooner or later have an effect on money prices. As John Locke (1632–1704) and Charles Davenant (1656–1714) pointed out, trade surpluses and the concomitant influx of precious metals eventually led to rising prices at home. Thus was born an early version of the "quantity theory of money," which envisions a link between the amount of money in circulation M and the price level P. If T is the transaction volume of goods in a single year and V the velocity of money's circulation, then it holds that $TP = MV$. If T and V can be viewed as given and constant, then the price level P increases proportionally with the money supply M.

Of course, mercantilists did not view the transaction volume as constant. Moderately rising prices were welcome as a sign of an economy that was picking up. What eluded the mercantilist authors, however, was the retroactive effects that rising prices at home had on the international competitiveness of domestic industry—and thus on the trade balance.

This connection was examined for the first time by the philosopher, historian, and economist David Hume (1711–1776) in his essays on economic matters. (Hume was a friend of Smith and like Smith was very critical of certain mercantilist ideas.) Hume drew attention to the price-specie flow mechanism, also known as gold "automatism": rising prices as a result of gold inflows diminish a country's competitiveness and tend to lead to a balanced trade. Hume also contradicted the mercantilist notion that one country can only win at the expense of other countries—a notion that explains the mercantilist focus on foreign trade and their neglect of domestic trade. In domestic trade, they believed, every winner was offset by a loser, whereas in foreign trade one country could win at the cost of other countries. (Today one would perhaps draw an analogy to a zero-sum game.) Hume disagreed: both foreign trade and domestic trade, he said, were potentially advantageous for all participants and enhanced their well-being.

National flavors of mercantilist thinking reflected differing economic and political conditions from country to country. In France, which was vying with England for supremacy, came Colbertism, named after Louis XIV's finance minister Jean-Baptiste Colbert (1619–1683). Colbert overhauled the government budget; reformed public administration; promoted French manufacturing to make the country independent of expensive imports; founded both the French East and West India Companies in pursuit of a colonial policy; expanded French infrastructure (streets, canals, ports); and brought foreign scientists, technicians, and skilled workers into the country to modernize the French economy. And like other mercantilists, he saw trade wars as an important source for increasing domestic stockpiles of precious metals.

Cameralism was the German variant of mercantilism, found in the small German states of the seventeenth century and especially in the eighteenth-century's era of enlightened absolutism. The term is derived from the treasure chamber (*camere*) of the prince. Essentially, cameralism was concerned with the art of governing a country efficiently and keeping the state's coffers full, as insurance against perils of all sorts. Cameralism's extensive literature dealt with constitutional and administrative law, public administration and accounting, and tax and fiscal policy. A properly functioning central administration, according to these thinkers, required civil servants trained in the cameral sciences and law. After the Thirty Years War (1618–1648), cameralists saw the immediate priority as rebuilding and settling the cities and villages that had been ravaged and depopulated, promoting agriculture, and encouraging population growth, with the long-term goal of developing the domestic economy by founding and promoting manufacturing and providing for public infrastructure. In all these activities, the cameralists viewed the state as an essential agent, either on its own or in cooperation with private enterprises. Major cameralist thinkers included Johann Joachim Becher (1635–1682), Philipp Wilhelm von Hörnigk (1640–1714), Johann Heinrich Gottlob von Justi (1717–1771), and Joseph von Sonnenfels (1732–1817).

2

CLASSICAL ECONOMICS

The first comprehensive investigation of the economic system came through "classical" economics during the Enlightenment in Europe. According to Karl Marx (1818–1883) and Joseph A. Schumpeter, William Petty (1623–1687) planted the seeds of the classical approach in the second half of the seventeenth century. Other important forerunners were Pierre Le Pesant de Boisguilbert (1646–1714), François Quesnay (1694–1774), and Anne-Robert-Jacques Turgot (1727–1781) in France; Richard Cantillon (1680–1734) and David Hume in Britain; and Antonio Genovesi (1713–1769), Ferdinando Galiani (1728–1787), Pietro Verri (1728–1797), and Cesare Beccaria (1738–1794) in Italy. British classical economics, on which I focus attention in the following, was in full bloom with Adam Smith and David Ricardo (1772–1823).

CHARACTERISTICS OF CLASSICAL THINKING

First, let me single out eight general features that characterize classical thinking. These concern:

1. the view that the economy is subject to laws that can be studied and then used to improve the conditions of life;
2. the stratification of society in social classes, whose members perform different roles in the economic process;

3. the conviction that large parts of economic activity can effectively be coordinated by means of interdependent markets, which leads to a new perspective on the role of the state in society;

4. the view that self-regarding actions of individuals typically have unintended consequences—a fact that is largely responsible for the extraordinary complexity of the subject of economics;

5. the conviction that in most nations the main lever of riches is labor—the skills, dexterity, and ingeniousness of the population—and that increases in labor productivity are due to ever-deeper social divisions of labor; correspondingly, the wealth of a nation is expressed in terms of the size of its social net product per capita;

6. the importance attributed to competition as a force that renders order and coherence to the economic system and fosters industry and technical progress, and the analysis of market-based economic coordination in competitive conditions leading to prices determined by cost of production;

7. the conception of a tendency toward a uniform rate of profits, resulting from the profit-seeking behavior of capital owners, and toward uniform rates of remuneration for the services of various qualities of land and labor, whose proprietors are in search of their most advantageous employments; and finally

8. the corresponding conception of the gravitation of market prices toward their "natural" levels, which reflect the general rate of profits and uniform wage rates and rent rates of the different kinds of work and qualities of land.

Let me expand on each of these a little further.

The first characteristic of the classical thinking is the conception that the economy obeys its own laws—laws that can be researched, understood, and used. Recent successes in the natural sciences provided a model for classical thinkers; Francis Bacon (1561–1626), for instance, had promoted the practical use of the natural sciences in the interest of social progress. In his book *Political Arithmetick* (1690), William Petty adopted the perspective of a physician who wished "to express my self in Terms of Number, Weight, or Measure; to use only Arguments of Sense, and to consider only such Causes, as have visible Foundations in Nature." Those causes "that depend upon the mutable Minds, Opinions, Appetites, and Passions of particular Men" he left to others. (In chap. 5 we will see that such cases are at the heart of marginalist value theory.) These economists saw their new science as quantitative and empirical; it must, according to François Quesnay, make use of mathematics and statistics. The classical economists were concerned with positive economics and with improving conditions through wise economic policy measures. Hence Smith (and Quesnay before him) conceived of the new discipline as an important, perhaps even the most important, part of a kind of master political science, encompassing what Smith called the "science of the legislator."

Second, classical thinkers saw as their subject of investigation an economy characterized by a growing division of labor and by private ownership of natural resources and the means of production, with the activities of its numerous economic agents coordinated via interconnected markets and with the exchange of goods and services facilitated by money serving as a means of exchange. Private agents were understood to interact in pursuit of their own goals and on their own account without (much) central guidance. Society was seen as divided into different classes, whose members performed different roles in the process of producing, distributing, and using society's wealth.

The classical economists emphasized the asymmetries between social classes in terms of differences in economic property and political power and access to information and knowledge. They would have met with disbelief the idea, popular in some parts of economics today, that an entire society can be understood by studying the behavior of a single "representative agent" only (see chaps. 4 and 10). People are different: their economic possibilities, motives, and mind-sets reflect their social backgrounds and how they were brought up. Society molds and changes people no less than people mold and change society. Classicists focused on a few key classes. There were the landlords who drew rent for leasing their land; as Smith put it in *The Wealth of Nations*, "they love to reap where they never sowed." Clinging to traditional feudal ways of life, landlords enjoyed lavish consumption based on this rent. They hardly saved or invested, and so they did not make a significant contribution to capital formation—the key to an increase in labor productivity. Workers owned almost nothing apart from their labor power. In order to support themselves and their families, they had to find employment at high enough wages. They spent their wages on food, clothes, and housing, and typically could not save much or at all. Capitalists or "masters" (Smith's term) were society's aspiring class. They had money and commercial capital (shops, means of transport, and merchandise) and means of production (plant and equipment) at their disposal. In an early stage of capitalism, the capitalists were also entrepreneurs—they started and ran businesses, meaning ownership and control were in the same hands. (Later, with the rise of joint-stock companies, management and control were increasingly turned over to managers, and the so-called principal-agent problem emerged: How can one make sure that the managers [the "agents"] act in the interest of the proprietors [the "principals"], and not merely in their own interests?) The income of capital owners was profit, the difference between sales revenues and production costs, and interest in the case of money capital. Capital owners were able to save and to invest in the development and modernization of the production apparatus, and competition provided strong incentives to do just that.

Third, classical economists repudiated the conviction acquired in Europe during the religious wars of the seventeenth century that if the system were left to itself it would inevitably sink into civil war. In *Leviathan* (1651), Thomas Hobbes (1588–1679) had argued that man in the state of nature has a natural right to everything and will, in light of his unbridled desires, become a rapacious wolf: *homo homini lupus est*. The state of nature leads unavoidably to a war of all against all (*bellum omnium contra omnes*). Leviathan, the absolutist state furnished with absolute power, ends the state of nature and brings about a condition of social equilibrium by keeping the "children of pride" in check.

No, the classical economists objected: a society in which large parts of economic activity are coordinated via interdependent markets based on free trade at home and abroad is (under certain circumstances) a self-regulating, homeostatic system. The concept of "equilibrium" thus found its way into the mental landscape of economists. Moreover, the classical economists argued that this kind of system facilitates a faster increase in the wealth of society than all other economic orders, because it stimulates hard work, business acumen, and inventiveness. The misgivings of Hobbes were seen as unfounded. *Laissez faire, laissez passer, le monde va de lui-même* (Let it be, let it alone, the world goes on by itself) was the famous call issued by economic liberalism. The conviction that a market economy not only works but can be expected to perform better than a centrally planned command economy or an economy with substantial government interferences had an important implication: it led to a redefinition of when economic affairs should be left to markets and when the government had a role to play in the economic process. While in feudal times subjects had to get permission from the kingly authority to engage in their businesses, now the government was asked to provide compelling reasons for its interference in the economic process, for the taxes it collected, its expenditures, and so on. The burden of proof was thus reversed.

The fourth leading idea of the classical economists, and one of the most important, is that human action typically leads to consequences neither intended nor planned nor foreseeable by the individual. As Adam Ferguson (1723–1816) succinctly put it: "History is the result of human action, but not the execution of any human design." Within the classical paradigm, individuals are seen as self-interested creatures with often complex motives. The ancestor of the fairly anemic figure of *homo economicus*—that self-interested actor so central to later economic thinking—appears on the stage in the writings of Quesnay. In this early formulation, he is somebody who wants to maximize his enjoyment (*jouissance*) and minimize his use of resources—a difficult task, as the only possible option is either maximizing or minimizing one of these quantities for a given level of the other one. Alas, it is an irremovable aspect of the human condition that humans only partly know and understand the world in which they live and can never be fully informed, and therefore time and again are bound to act in ways that generate effects that were no part of their plans. Some of these effects may affect the well-being of others, for better or worse.

Humans are not isolated individuals like Robinson Crusoe on his island (before he met Friday). On the island no other party is involved, and Robinson could fully concentrate on his relationship with the material world around himself, using the means at his disposal as best as he could to satisfy his needs and wants. Not so in the economy studied by the classical economists. Recognizing that different agents and branches of the economy are mutually dependent on one another, these economists started to see the *interdependence* of economic units as a central analytical theme. The task of political economy was to analyze the entanglement of intended and unintended consequences that resulted from the actions of self-regarding agents. In particular, the goal was to figure out which actions and behaviors had not just private but socially beneficial results—and which actions, while privately beneficial, were socially harmful. This in turn meant combating superstition, exuberance, and hysteria in social and economic matters and suggesting social institutions, incentives, laws, and a regulatory framework that supported beneficial behaviors and contained those that were harmful. Political economy was thus seen to have an eminently practical relevance.

A fifth characteristic of the classical economists' thinking was the conviction that the main source of a large and growing wealth of most nations was neither the colonization of other countries and exploitation of their resources nor favorable overseas trade ("buy cheaply, sell dearly"). The main source, instead, consisted of the industry and diligence of the working population—in short, labor and production—and an increasing labor productivity. The classical authors no longer measured wealth in terms of a given stock of gold and silver in the king's coffers at a given moment of time but in terms of the net *flow* of commodities produced during a year. In this way they anticipated the modern concept of net domestic product: a nation is the richer the larger its net social product per capita—that is, its gross domestic product (GDP) less all the goods which of necessity have to be used up in the course of production (raw materials, tools, and machines, but also the necessary upkeep of the workforce). Quesnay talked about the *"produit net,"* Adam Smith and David Ricardo about a "surplus product" or "neat produce." A characteristic feature of the analyses of the classical authors is that they counted the means of subsistence that productive workers needed to survive and reproduce as a part of the necessary yearly advances and thus of the indispensable physical real costs of production— on a par with the feed for the cattle and the fuel for the engines. (In contemporary national accounting, the wages of labor are instead reckoned in their entirety among the net social product.)

The focus was on commodities that could be produced and reproduced, like wheat, bread, iron, tools, machines, and so on. (Nonreproducible goods such as fine art, for example, were dealt with only in passing.) Reproduction was a twin concept of surplus. An economic system is said to be able to reproduce itself if it is able to produce, year after year, at least as much as it necessarily uses up in production and thus "destroys" or "consumes productively" (this includes the means of production and means of subsistence). A major concern of economic policy was to increase the social surplus by avoiding waste, increasing efficiency, and raising labor productivity. In systems that generate a surplus, the question is always how to use the surplus: it can either be consumed or saved and invested (that is, accumulated). In the latter case the economy will grow, markets will expand, the division of labor will deepen, and productivity will grow. Hence the classical economists' concern with the size, and growing size, of the surplus.

But how does a private-decentralized system in which the coordination of millions of independently taken decisions and actions is left to markets function? This brings us to the sixth characteristic of the classical economists' point of view, which revolves around the concepts of free competition, a tendency toward a uniform rate of profits, and the corresponding gravitation of market prices to their natural levels. The classical economists had to show that pursuing agents' self-interest in a decentralized economy through a network of interdependent markets did not imply anarchy and chaos, as several economists and social philosophers had argued. No Leviathan was required, and if there was one it was detrimental to the well-being of the large majority of the people. At the heart of classical economics, therefore, was an explanation of market-mediated coordination, price formation, and the resultant income distribution.

In the perspective of the classical authors, prices reflect the difficulty of producing the various commodities, that is, the costs incurred in overcoming the obstacles to obtain them. The amount of labor needed both directly and indirectly (in producing intermediate products, such as raw materials and means of production) was considered a good measure of this difficulty. Hence most classical economists advocated some sort of labor theory of value, according to which the total amount of labor "embodied" in a commodity held the key to its value or price. Most also understood, albeit with different degrees of sophistication, that the time profile of the labor spent producing a commodity mattered in ascertaining the commodity's value. For instance, if most of the total labor embodied in a commodity is expended early in its production, this implies that most wages were paid a long time before the completion of the product. At a positive rate of profits this sum has to be discounted forward at compound rate and covered by the price of the product. Hence two commodities produced with exactly the same amount of total labor will nevertheless have different prices, if the time profiles of the corresponding streams of labor expenditures differ. In this more general perspective, "natural prices" express two causes instead of only one: the methods of production used in producing the various commodities (reflected in the overall amount and time profiles of labor expenditures) and income distribution, that is, the level of real wages (and the corresponding level of the general rate of profits). While the former cause expresses the level of technical and organizational knowledge at a given time and place, the latter reflects the balance of power in the "dispute" (as Adam Smith put it) over the distribution of income. Competitive conditions are seen to enforce cost-minimizing behavior of firms.

Seventh, classical economic thinking understood competition as rivalry among agents on both sides of the market—that is among suppliers and demanders. Firms, for example, compete with one another for the largest possible sales volume and market share. Competition assumes that control over an object is not monopolized but instead spread out among several agents. The medieval guild system, a serf's servile obligation to work the land on a feudal estate, or a monopoly granted by princely favor all hindered the mobility of labor and capital and shielded abnormally high incomes from competition. In today's vocabulary, such markets were not "contestable." The classical authors showed how monopolies, privileges, and impediments to mobility for manpower and capital in general were advantageous to some and disadvantageous to many.

The ideal as Smith saw it was free competition—the absence of noticeable barriers to market entry and exit. Free competition, the classical thinkers were convinced, ensures coherence and order and spurs the development of labor productivity. It works like an "invisible hand," as Smith famously put it, and takes the place of the visible hand of the state. As a social institution, free competition would reward and punish without requiring a Leviathan. It makes use of man's self-interest. If there is a shortage of supply of a good in a market, competition among demanders forces up the market price. This increases profit margins, attracting capital and labor from other branches and finally leading to an increase in the output and supply of the good under consideration. This in turn causes the market price to fall again. The converse would apply in the case of an excess supply of a good.

The restless search of capital owners for the highest possible profits per unit of capital invested and of workers for the highest possible wages would lead to a general rate of profits or rate of return on capital that tends to be uniform across all branches of the economy and to equal wages for equal work. Both classical (and postclassical) economic thinking revolved around the determination of the general rate of profits and its movement over time. As Marx would later articulate in *Capital*, the rate of profits is a key figure in the system, "the stimulus . . . as also the driving force for accumulation." Investment happens in expectation of profits, and investments are financed not least out of profits. If the rate of profits falls, the inclination to form new capital weakens, and economic growth runs dry.

Finally, eighth, alongside the concept of a general rate of profits was a corresponding concept of "natural" or "production" prices. These were seen to reflect systematic and permanent forces at work, while "market" prices reflected a multitude of incidental and temporary factors (e.g., the weather) on top of that. Competition causes market prices to gravitate toward or oscillate around production prices, so the former never stray too far from the latter. Only by way of production prices, the classical economists insisted, could generalizable statements be formed, and so their focus was on understanding such prices. These prices and the corresponding distributive variables—the general rate of profits, real wages, and the rents of land—were bound to change in the course of time as capital accumulated, the population grew, natural resources became scarce, and new technical and organizational knowledge filtered into the economic system. The classical authors sought to study economic development in terms of a sequence of long-period positions of the economic system, each one characterized by particular levels of prices, the rate of profits, wages, and rents.

Let us conclude this section by illustrating the links connecting wages, profits, and natural prices, as Smith and Ricardo discussed them, in terms of an exceedingly simple example known as the wheat model (the "corn" model in British English). In this model, production takes place in two sectors: agriculture and manufacturing. For simplicity's sake, we ignore ground rent—the rent paid for the use of land on which the wheat is grown. (We thus implicitly assume that land of best quality is available in abundance.) Wheat is produced in the agricultural sector by means of wheat (seed), and in the manufacturing sector is distilled into whiskey for the well-to-do classes of society. Wheat is used to feed workers, as seed in agriculture and as a raw material in industry. It therefore goes directly into the production of all products, including itself. "Wheat" is a collective term for all the foodstuffs or necessaries of the workers. Everywhere it is indispensable as an input, because work is employed everywhere. Real wages paid in any one of the two sectors are equal to the total number of hours worked there during a year, times the amount of wheat paid to workers per hour. "Whiskey" on the other hand is, accordingly, a collective term for all of the consumer goods defined as "luxuries"; nowhere does it go into production as a necessary input.

Deducting the total expenditure on wheat (which is equal to the capital employed in seed and food to feed the workers) from the annual gross output of wheat gives us the net output of wheat. This net output constitutes the profits of farmers (that is, the tenants of land). The ratio of profits to the capital employed is equal to the profit rate earned in agriculture. In the manufacturing sector, a share of the net output of wheat is used to hire workers and as a raw material processed into whiskey. In conditions of free competition whiskey producers will obtain the same rate of profits as farmers. This means that the price for the volume of whiskey produced is equal to the wheat (or the capital) employed in its production, plus the profit at the uniform rate. But this rate, as we have seen, has already been determined in the agricultural sector. Thus, given technical conditions of production in agriculture and in the manufacturing sector and the real wage rate in terms of wheat, one can determine the general rate of profits and the price of whiskey relative to that of wheat. (The analysis can easily be extended to the case in which there are more than just two products.)

The classical economists therefore established the rate of profit and prices in an economy at a given time by proceeding from the following data (or given or independent variables): (1) the gross output of the different goods produced, (2) the available technology that allows producers to transform inputs into outputs, and (3) the prevailing real wage. Profits and wages are determined *asymmetrically*: wages are assumed as known when the issue is the size of the profit rate. The level of the wage rate is then examined in another part of the analysis when considering capital accumulation, technical progress, and population growth. Over time, the profit rate, wages, and prices are bound to change as the variables 1–3 change.

This is the surplus theory approach taken by classical economics, which differs fundamentally from the later marginalist approach (see chap. 5).

FRANÇOIS QUESNAY We have to thank Louis XV's mistress Madame de Pompadour for assisting her personal physician Quesnay in printing the results of an epoch-making discovery—the *Tableau Économique* (1756). In a single picture, analogous to a mechanical clock, Quesnay depicted production, distribution, and utilization of an entire nation's social wealth. Production, as he diagrammed it, takes place in two sectors—agriculture and industry—which depend on each other. In exchange for money, agriculture supplies industry with raw materials and means of subsistence, while industry supplies agriculture with equipment (plows, other instruments of production, etc.).

Quesnay called those working in agriculture the "productive class" and those working in industry the "sterile class." The first is productive because it produces more wheat than it uses up (seed plus means of sustenance). Its net product he considered to be a "pure gift of nature"—nature works together with men, but it supplies its services for free. Hence the name "physiocracy" for his economic theory, meaning the rule of nature. The second class is sterile, because it merely processes a part of this net product into other forms (for example, wheat into whiskey) without adding anything to it. The landowning class (king, nobility, clergy) obtains a rent from tenants that is equal in value to the net product in agriculture. Landowners use this rent in part to buy means of subsistence for themselves, domestic servants, civil servants, and the military, and the rest is used to purchase industrial products (luxury consumer goods, weapons, coaches, etc.). The prices of products cover all costs, and for the prices of agricultural products this includes the lease or ground rent. (Profits play no explicit role in Quesnay's construction; they are subsumed under the incomes of tenants and independent artisans.) Society's net income, accordingly, is equal to the sum total of the rents paid to landowners. According to Quesnay rent was the only income that should be taxed (*impôt unique*), because all other incomes are taken to cover barely more than just the living costs of their recipients—a proposal that did not earn physiocrats the sympathy of the king and the landed gentry.

ADAM SMITH ON THE "INVISIBLE HAND" With *An Inquiry into the Nature and Causes of the Wealth of Nations* (abbreviated henceforth as *The Wealth of Nations*), first published in 1776 with four more editions to follow, the Scotsman Adam Smith permanently shaped the new field of political economy, both thematically and methodologically, and won it an important place in the circle of the venerable sciences. No metaphor of Smith's is as well known as that of the "invisible hand," and none has been so fundamentally misunderstood.

Many have attributed to Smith the extreme view that selfish behavior of whatever kind unequivocally results in unintended consequences that are beneficial to society as a whole. In this perspective nothing but selfishness is needed for societies to achieve optimal outcomes. But it was not Smith who held this view. It was instead the satirist and cynic Bernard Mandeville (1670–1733) who proclaimed this doctrine in his famous *Fable of the Bees* (1705). Both Smith and David Hume before him disagreed with Mandeville and in his *Theory of Moral Sentiments* (1759) Smith called the latter's views "in almost every respect erroneous." Not virtue but vice is the actual source of the common good, Mandeville had contended. How could Adam Smith, author of a widely praised investigation into the sources and development of morality and ethics, adhere to such an abstruse idea? Whether deliberately or out of ignorance, others have contended Smith held a view to which he was uncompromisingly opposed, as his attack on the mercantilist system shows. He saw this system's "principal architects" as money- and power-hungry merchants, possessed by "the wretched spirit of monopoly," whose main goal was to procure individual advantages at the expense of the general public.

So what does the metaphor of the invisible hand really imply? In *The Wealth of Nations* we read this about the individual: "By pursuing his own interest he frequently promotes that of the society more effectually than when he really intends to promote it." *Frequently*, not always. In order for the pursuit of self-interest to promote rather than damage the general interest, Smith insisted, certain institutional preconditions need to be met. As the Smith scholar Edwin Cannan wrote: "The working of self-interest is generally beneficent, not because of some natural coincidence between the self-interest of each and the good of all, but *because human institutions are arranged so as to compel self-interest to work in directions in which it will be beneficent*" (emphasis added). It was the task of the statesman to create the kinds of institutions and laws that made it in the interest even of bad people to act for the good of all. The science of the legislator, Smith elaborated, was designed to show the way to good government.

ADAM SMITH ON THE DIVISION OF LABOR For Adam Smith, the division of labor was the most important source of growth in labor productivity and per capita income. Initially, he argued, there was a division of labor within and then between firms and regions in a given country, and finally between countries. Smith was an eloquent advocate of free trade and what today is called "globalization." But his advocacy was tied to an important condition: the advantages of free trade had to accrue to the benefit of *all* countries and parties involved, which again points to the importance of good government. (We return to this issue later.)

The division of labor (1) yields gains from specialization, (2) saves time that is lost in changing from one task or job to another, and most importantly, (3) promotes the development of machines. Labor power is replaced by machine power, and production is mechanized—a process for which there is no end in sight.

New trades and occupations emerge, including "that of those who are called philosophers or men of speculation, whose trade it is, not to do any thing, but to observe every thing; and who, upon that account, are often capable of combining together the powers of the most distant and dissimilar objects. In the progress of society, philosophy or speculation becomes, like every other employment, the principal or sole trade and occupation of a particular class of citizens." Today we call this research and development (R&D). The new knowledge that is systematically produced enables "improvements" in production and organization. Two centuries before the emergence of the concept of a "knowledge society," Smith had already explicitly identified the "quantity of science" as the foundation of society's productive powers.

The motor of the wealth-producing machine, Smith insisted, was capital accumulation. It set in motion a "virtuous circle": by enlarging markets, capital accumulation facilitated a deeper division of labor, which led to higher productivity and as a consequence to higher profits and incomes more generally, leading in turn to further capital accumulation, and so on and so forth. There emerges the picture of an incessant upward spiral: capital accumulation is both the source and the effect of the continual transformation to which the market system is subjected—the process is characterized by "cumulative causation," change feeds on itself.

Economic policy had to set the overall framework. Smith was convinced that the mercantile system of monopolies, import restrictions, and export promotion led to a misguided allocation of resources, dampened economic dynamism, and had unwanted distributional effects. It went against the liberal principles of "equality [in the sense of equal rights], liberty, and justice." Smith was especially hard on the mercantilist promotion of cities (and therewith of industry) and foreign trade. This went against the "natural course of things," in which agriculture is the first sector to develop, followed by industry and cities in tandem with domestic trade, and foreign commerce only in a final stage. Agriculture is said to have the highest added value, since in that sector "nature labours along with man" and "costs no expense." This physiocratic idea would later be subjected to persuasive critique by Ricardo. But foreign trade, although it offered opportunities for higher profits, also harbored higher risks and greater insecurity for capital investment, according to Smith. The risk-averse capital owner therefore preferred to invest at home and, in pursuing his own advantage there, provided for higher domestic employment and income: "He is . . . led by an invisible hand to promote an end which was no part of his intention."

ADAM SMITH ON WAGES, PROFITS, AND RENT With regard to the distribution of income, Adam Smith saw interests in conflict with one another and unequal negotiating power at work. "The workmen desire to get as much, the masters to give as little, as possible." He named three disadvantages for workers: their large numbers made it hard to organize their interests, the law did not allow them to collude and strike, and they could not hold out very long in labor disputes for lack of wherewithal. The wages for simple work therefore tended to reach a level that just barely enabled the workers and their families to survive and reproduce. Only if capital accumulated rapidly and the demand for labor grew faster than the supply would employers breach their agreement not to raise wages. Since, according to Smith, "no society can surely be flourishing and happy, of which the far greater part of the members are poor and miserable," he was interested in this rapid capital accumulation: it improved the lot of the "labouring poor," the happiness of the greatest number. To be sure, higher wages led—owing to better nourishment, lower mortality, and growing birthrates—to accelerated population growth, so the rise in wages was moderated again. With these observations Smith anticipated an element of the population theory published in 1798 by Thomas Robert Malthus (1766–1834) in *An Essay on the Principle of Population*. However, while Malthus was convinced that "the power of population is indefinitely greater than the power in the earth to produce subsistence for man," with the result that population was constantly in danger of being checked by famines, Smith was not pessimistic about economic development. The economic system Smith envisaged could produce from within (endogenously) the working population required for the accumulation of capital. In his view there was no permanent discrepancy between the increase of population on the one hand and the provision of food on the other, as Malthus was to argue.

Profits (and rents), according to Smith, were pure property incomes and not "the wages of a particular sort of labour, the labour of inspection and direction." With a uniform profit rate in a competitive economy, the individual capital owner partakes in total profits in the same way that a stockholder shares in distributed dividends—each one sharing in relation to the size of his capital. Smith believed that the general rate of profits had a tendency to fall in the long run. His reasoning, however, is not tenable. He was misled by generalizing an observation that applies to a single sector in the economy to the economy as a whole. If capital flows from one sector of the economy into another in search of a higher return on capital, then production will decrease in the former and increase in the latter. Correspondingly, but conversely, prices will increase in the former and decrease in the latter. In the sector into which capital flows profitability will fall because of falling prices. Smith appears to have had only this latter case in mind when he argued that the increase of capital in the system as a whole will "intensify competition" and thus bring down the rate of profit. But first, since he assumed free competition in the first place, competition can hardly intensify. And second, while the rate of profit in the latter sector tends to fall, the rate of profit in the former tends to rise. The overall rate of profit in the system as a whole will thus largely remain constant. It follows that capital accumulation can only lead to a fall in the general rate of profits if either the real wage rate rises, other things being equal, or less and less fertile natural resources have to be utilized, given the real wage rate. It was Ricardo who criticized and corrected Smith's mistaken doctrine of the falling tendency of the rate of profits.

Smith developed a highly interesting theory of wage and profit rate differentials. Using factors like the convenience or inconvenience of a business—an extreme case Smith cites is that of the public executioner—or its inherent risks and the costs of learning a profession (human capital), he attempted to explain why wages and profit rates differed from one business to another. The productivity of the worker, according to this view, is just one of several factors in wage determination. Thus, for example, a public executioner earns extraordinarily well, given that he is employed only sporadically; the inconvenience of his job, being shunned by the community, obtains him a high compensation. Smith compares incomes in a number of professions (lawyers and physicians, for instance) to lotteries: the winner gets a lot, the loser only a little. He anticipated the basic idea of "efficiency wages" (see chap. 10): abnormally high wages should prevent employees from shirking or even sabotaging the production process, because losing their jobs would be very costly for them.

Smith calls profit (and interest) a "deduction" from the product of labor. This echoes some of the Aristotelian contempt for interest. But unlike a long-standing tradition in moral philosophy, Smith saw profit (and interest) as socially acceptable—and this reinterpretation of the ethical status of profits represents what is perhaps Smith's greatest achievement on behalf of the postfeudal, capitalist economic and social order. The rising class of capital owners was, admittedly, egoistic and greedy. To this extent, the old moral judgment could not be denied. But, Smith argued, it fell short. If one judges people not according to their intentions but rather for what they can bring about in a (well-governed!) society, then a different picture emerges. With appropriate institutions and policies, Smith held that self-regard and even egoism promotes the general good.

ADAM SMITH ON THE ROLE OF THE STATE AND TAXES Smith differentiated, in a new way, between the subareas of economic activity that should be reserved for the state and those that should be left to the private sector. The state, according to his view, should only take on tasks that private agents either are incapable of carrying out or cannot do as well as government can (or can do only at a higher cost). Once the legitimate tasks of the state are fixed, the means to finance them must be decided. According to Smith, the maxim to follow is that the private sector should not be burdened with excessive taxation.

Smith's remarks on this matter are frequently interpreted as a plea for a "minimal" or "night watchman state." This interpretation is untenable. *The Wealth of Nations* includes an impressive set of regulatory tasks for the state. Indeed, Smith was concerned with transforming the old authoritarian state into a modern constitutional and achievement-oriented state that reacts appropriately to the changing needs of the day. Smith recognized, for instance, that the division of labor could have negative by-products: the devaluation of artisanal skills and the replacement of adult with child labor. He called for state-financed elementary school education to cushion the negative consequences of this development. He listed other responsibilities of the state, including the administration of justice, policing, and national defense; the provision of infrastructure to facilitate the movement of people and goods; and the organization of large-scale projects in the general interest. In light of historical experiences—especially the introduction on a large scale of paper money in France at the beginning of the eighteenth century and the ensuing Mississippi Bubble—Smith also advocated regulating the unstable banking sector, since "those exertions of the natural liberty of a few individuals, which might endanger the security of the whole society, are, and ought to be, restrained by the laws of all governments." And while he considered paper money on a par with technical progress, because it allowed a society to save on the costly provision of gold and silver, he warned that the commerce and industry of a country "cannot be altogether so secure, when they are thus, as it were, suspended upon the *Daedalian wings of paper money*" (emphasis added). According to Greek mythology, Daedalus was a gifted craftsman who built wings of wax and feathers with which he and his son Icarus escaped from the island of Crete after having been imprisoned by Minos. But hubris—or should we say "irrational exuberance"?—made Icarus ignore his father's warnings: he got too close to the sun, which made the wax in his wings melt, and he fell into the sea and died.

Taxes should be proportionally equal, according to Smith, who thus addressed both the ability-to-pay principle (that taxation should be based on income) and the equivalence principle (that taxation should be based on the benefits experienced as a result of government activity).

DAVID RICARDO Starting out as a highly successful stockjobber on the London Exchange—on the occasion of Napoleon's defeat at the Battle of Waterloo in 1815, he made an enormous fortune—Ricardo came to political economy by reading *The Wealth of Nations*. The topic became his "most favourite subject." His first publishing in the area was about monetary and currency questions. He wrote, for instance, that the rise of the price level between 1797 and 1821 was above all the result of overactive money printing. In the so-called bullionist controversy, he took the side of the bullionists, who called for a quick return to the gold standard. Such a move, they argued, would ensure that a rising price level at home (relative to abroad) would lead, via commodity and capital flows, to a devaluation of the currency and so result in purchasing power parity between currencies at home and abroad.

Ricardo, a man of considerable practical sense, defended economic theory against the "vulgar charge" made by people who are "all for fact and nothing for theory. Such men can hardly ever sift their facts. They are credulous, and necessarily so, because they have no standard of reference." Nothing, said Ricardo, is more practical than a good theory, thus confirming a wisdom of Immanuel Kant's! He was one of the first economists to investigate the workings of the economic world by means of small models that got to the core of each specific problem and were intended to lay a foundation for economic policy recommendations. Schumpeter talks about the "Ricardian vice"—a vice to which he and all of economics succumb. Models are always, in light of the subject's complexity, insufficiently complex. The only interesting thing is whether or not they provide insights that enhance our understanding. In Ricardo's case, they typically do.

RICARDO'S THEORY OF VALUE AND DISTRIBUTION Ricardo was fascinated by Smith's analysis, but he found several weaknesses that needed to be rectified. He did so in his *Principles of Political Economy and Taxation*, first published in 1817 and followed by two other editions. With this book, according to John Maynard Keynes (1883–1946), Ricardo "conquered England as completely as the Holy Inquisition conquered Spain." This is certainly an exaggeration, but Ricardo's long-term impact is considerable. Smith had maintained in *The Wealth of Nations* that only "in that early and rude state of society which precedes both the accumulation of stock and the appropriation of land" did the amount of labor directly deployed in production determine the relative prices of two products. Ricardo objected. He held that the labor theory of value is also applicable, at least approximately, when workers use tools (capital goods, like a trap for catching beaver or a spear in a deer hunt)—only now the *indirect* labor performed in generating such tools (the trap, the spear) has to be added to the *direct* labor of trapping or hunting. The level of total labor expended is a gauge measuring the "difficulty of production." Technical progress reduces this difficulty and is reflected in lower labor values for commodities. Ricardo's basic message proved to be perfectly true: the higher labor productivity is, the less "expensive" commodities are in terms of the total labor needed to produce them, and the more wealthy a nation is.

Smith, insisted Ricardo, had also failed to recognize that the real wage rate and the profit rate had an *inverse* relationship with each other for a given state of technology. Ricardo's fundamental law of income distribution says: "The greater the portion of the result of labour that is given to the labourer, the smaller must be the rate of profits, and vice versa."

To Ricardo it was clear that, in general, a change in income distribution has an impact on the relative prices of commodities, because their production exhibits different proportions of direct labor to indirect labor needed to produce the necessary intermediate products (remember the reference to different time profiles earlier). Commodities produced with relatively large labor inputs (and thus large wage payments) in early stages of production will imply higher prices relative to products made with relatively small labor inputs in early stages when the rate of profits is higher (and the wage rate correspondingly lower). This is so because of the compound interest effect: at a higher rate of profits, discounting forward relatively large wage payments in an early stage of the production process renders these commodities relatively more expensive. Yet Ricardo did not succeed in fully grasping the dependence of relative prices on income distribution, given the technology used, and for a lack of a better theory adhered to the labor theory of value, because it seemed approximately correct to him.

RICARDO'S THEORY OF GROUND RENT Especially unsuccessful, according to Ricardo, was Smith's explanation of ground rent as an expression of the "fertility of nature." Quite the contrary, Ricardo insisted: rent is an expression of how nature is "niggardly"! If land of the best quality and location were available in unlimited quantity, he expounded, there would be no ground rent, because cost-minimizing producers would be able to satisfy society's need for wheat at every level by using only this kind of land. But because this kind of land is not available in abundance but becomes *scarce* at some point as production expands, it is necessary to meet demand by also cultivating inferior land, which exhibits higher unit cost of production, or by cultivating the best quality of land more intensively, which is also only possible at a rising unit cost. As a result, returns fall either extensively or intensively, leading to extensive or intensive rents.

If, for example, demand is large and cultivation is expanded on parcels of inferior land, production costs per quarter of wheat will be higher. In order for the larger quantity to be brought forth the wheat price will accordingly have to rise. The higher price for wheat enables the owners of the superior quality land—who continue to produce at lower unit cost—to collect a rent from their tenants that is just large enough to result in equal costs (inclusive of rent) on both pieces of land. In this new situation, no rent is paid on the inferior land, which is not scarce and which represents marginal land in the given situation. Ground rent is therefore a differential rent attributable to differences in production costs per quarter of wheat. To Ricardo, trained in the financial markets, the connection between the annual rent per hectare of a piece of land of given quality j, r_j, and the land price per hectare, p_j, was clear. If one discounts all future annual rent payments at the prevailing interest rate i in order to get their so-called present or capital value, one arrives at the formula for the eternal rent: $p_j = r_j/i$. If the lease is, for example, £100 and the interest rate 4 percent (or 0.04), the price per hectare of that land amounts to £2,500.

With society's growing need for wheat, and setting aside technological progress, the unit cost of wheat would rise, as would prices and ground rents. Thus, for a given real wage rate, there necessarily ensues a falling rate of profit for producers in agriculture and in the economy as a whole. This was Ricardo's explanation for the tendency of the rate of profit to fall. He is now often seen, therefore, as a pessimist about progress. This is a misinterpretation. For Ricardo, a falling rate of profits was the logical outcome only in the hypothetical case where there was no technological progress. But since technological progress does exist, "it is difficult to say where the limit is at which you would cease to accumulate wealth, and to derive profit from its employment." Ricardo clearly did not share Malthus's pessimism as regards the possibilities of bettering mankind's lot!

Ricardo was able to put this theory to lucrative use; drawing concrete conclusions from his ideas, he used a large part of the fortune he had gained following the Battle of Waterloo to purchase land and became one of England's wealthiest landowners. His calculation: should the accelerating accumulation of capital and the ensuing shortage of lands following Waterloo mean that the lease on the land in the above-mentioned example rose to £150, and the interest rate (as a result of the tendency of the profit rate to fall) sink to 3 percent (or 0.03), the price of land would rise to £5,000. His calculation paid off.

"SAY'S LAW" Like Smith before him, Ricardo held the view that "there is no amount of capital which may not be employed in a country, because demand is only limited by production." There will always, in other words, be sufficient demand for commodities to ensure the full use of the capital stock. In a famous debate, he contradicted Malthus, who had contended that a "general glut" of commodities—an excess of output as a whole over aggregate effective demand—was possible. The two agreed that savings meant a loss of demand for goods and that each saving would be followed by an equally large investment. Investments mean demand for commodities—compensating for each loss of demand due to savings. How then, asked Ricardo, could Malthus claim that the economy could be constrained from the demand side?

The resulting view that the economic system can never be demand constrained entered the literature as "Say's law," named after the French economist Jean-Baptiste Say (1767–1832). The classical economists applied the "law" only to commodities produced with the intention of making profits, not to labor. Only later would the law be extended to the labor market and so imply the thesis of a tendency to full employment. Nothing of the sort is found in Ricardo. Indeed, in the third edition of his *Principles* (1821), impressed by the protest movement of the Luddites, who were convinced that the misery of the workers was due to the labor-displacing effects of machines, he added a new chapter "On Machinery" and showed how the replacement of labor by machine power can lead to lasting unemployment.

RICARDO'S THEORY OF COMPARATIVE ADVANTAGE IN FOREIGN TRADE Ricardo regarded Smith's explanation of how countries specialize based on absolute advantages in production costs for specific goods as incomplete. Assume, he argued, that the home country can produce all goods at lower costs than can be done abroad. Then, initially, it is only the home country that exports goods, which foreign countries import. This leads to an inflow of gold (the money commodity) at home and to an outflow from abroad (Hume's price-specie flow mechanism). According to the quantity theory of money, prices rise at home and fall abroad. At some point the prices of some commodities abroad fall below those at home, so that the absolute cost advantage reverses itself, and the foreign countries can now export the commodities under consideration. Which commodities does this affect?

Ricardo developed the "principle of comparative advantage" as an answer. Take, he expounded, the example of trade in cloth and wine between England and Portugal. Assume that, in Portugal, 90 hours of labor are needed to produce a bale of cloth and 80 hours for a cask of wine. In England, meanwhile, it takes 100 hours for cloth and 120 hours for wine. Portugal possesses an absolute advantage with respect to both products, and with respect to wine also a comparative (relative) advantage: the cost difference for wine (80/120) is greater than for cloth (90/100). (Correspondingly England faces an absolute disadvantage with respect to both products but a comparative advantage with respect to cloth.) For Portuguese producers, it is worthwhile to specialize in the production and export of wine while importing cloth from England, where the English absolute disadvantage is comparatively small.

We may explain Ricardo's important principle, which Nobel laureate Paul A. Samuelson (1915–2009) called both "true" and "nontrivial," in another way, drawing attention to the involved possibility of "arbitrage," meaning here the exploitation of price differences in the two countries involved. Assume that the two countries have their own currencies, which are supposed to be nonconvertible—Portugal the Portuguese real and

TABLE 2.1. Price in Reals (Portugal) and Pounds (England)
of Given Quantities of Cloth and Wine

	CLOTH	WINE
In Portugal (Reals)	90	80
In England (Pounds)	100	120

England the pound. Assume that the money prices of the quantities of cloth and wine in the two countries are proportional to the quantities of labor spent in producing them, and assume for simplicity that the numbers are the same, the only difference being that now, instead of Portuguese and English labor, we have reals and pounds (table 2.1).

One can easily see that trade would be favorable to merchants of both countries. (In the following, for simplicity, we set aside transportation costs.) Take the case of an English merchant. He may buy for £100 a given quantity of cloth, ship it to Portugal, and sell it there for 90 reals. With this sum of money he may then buy wine from a Portuguese wine grower and get altogether $90/80 = 9/8$ units of wine, where one unit costs 80 reals. This quantity of wine he then ships to England and sells for $9/8 \times £120 = £135$. He thus yields a profit of £135 − £100 = £35 or a rate of profit of 35 percent on an investment of £100 over the time it took to export cloth and import wine. (It deserves to be noted that the English merchant can use the same ship to export and import goods from and to England.) A similar consideration applies to a Portuguese merchant.

The remarkable fact here is (as opposed to the previous explanation with gold as the universal means of payment) that while goods are exported and imported, the currencies of the two countries do not cross borders: they stay in the countries of origin; there are no flows of money into and out of a country.

What applies to specialization between countries also applies to trade between people. The happy message of Ricardo's finding is this: whoever is inferior to another person in everything can nonetheless become involved in a division of labor that is mutually advantageous. In this way, Ricardo added an important verse to Adam Smith's hymn of praise on the beneficent effects of the division of labor.

JOHN STUART MILL Although Mill (1806–1873) saw himself as merely correcting and completing the Ricardian doctrine, he was really a transitional figure, foreshadowing certain elements of the later marginalist doctrine (see chap. 4). His *Principles of Political Economy with Some of Their Applications to Social Philosophy*, first published in 1848, became one of the most successful overviews of the field altogether, and only in 1890 was it superseded by Alfred Marshall's (1842–1924) *Principles*. Here we touch only upon a few of his ideas and concepts.

Mill's turn away from Ricardo is demonstrated most clearly in his explanation of profits. According to his "abstinence theory," saving involves an "abstinence from present consumption" and ought to be considered a "sacrifice" that is compensated for by profit (or interest). While Ricardo had explained profits in objective terms, Mill introduced a subjective element. Critics objected that "abstinence" cannot be clearly measured and asked why it should be considered a sacrifice. A millionaire who saves some income can hardly be said to abstain from consumption. Critics of Mill also maintained that, in terms of such subjective notions, anything and the opposite of it may be established, adding that such explanations could easily be employed for purely apologetic purposes.

For a while, Mill also advocated the so-called wages-fund theory, which was a primitive anticipation of extending Say's law to the labor market. The idea is as follows: In a given year, a fixed quantity of food is available to employ labor, which is called the wages-fund F. A flexible wage rate w is taken to adapt to this such that all N job seekers also find employment. The equation that obtains is $w = F/N$ or $F = wN$. For a given F, this expression can also be interpreted as a rudimentary demand function for labor: the higher w is, the lower N is, and vice versa. But the idea expressed this way is not convincing: neither can the wages-fund F be viewed as a constant, nor are wages downwardly flexible to any level, and even if they were, the existing physical capital stock (machines, buildings) could not employ an arbitrary number of workers. Mill later admitted that the wages-fund theory was untenable and retracted it.

In foreign trade theory, Mill maintained that Ricardo's analysis was incomplete, because it did not explain the amounts of commodities produced, exported, and imported by a country. He sought to supplement the Ricardian doctrine with a theory of demand.

As a utilitarian, he saw rising income as accompanied by falling marginal utility (each additional dollar brings an ever-smaller increase in utility). He therefore advocated income and inheritance taxation to diminish inequality. For Mill, the liberal, a large inequality in incomes and wealth spells trouble for the principle of equal opportunities of the young, favoring the offspring of the "haves" and discriminating against those of the "have-nots." The task of an inheritance taxation was to get the system closer to equal opportunities without suffocating industry and business acumen.

DEVELOPMENT OF THE CLASSICAL APPROACH Classical economic theory lived on in many forms and configurations and had a major impact on the development of economics. The classical theory of value and distribution was picked up with critical intent by Marx and attacked at roughly the same time by representatives of the rising marginalist school (see chapters 3 and 4). Toward the end of the nineteenth century, the Russian economist Vladimir K. Dmitriev (1868–1913) formalized parts of Ricardo's doctrine. Ladislaus von Bortkiewicz (1868–1931), who taught in Berlin, built on Dmitriev's work. In 1937 the Hungarian mathematician and natural scientist Janos (later John) von Neumann (1903–1957), apparently unaware of the classical works, published a model of economic growth that exhibits genuinely classical features.

The most important contribution to the development of classical theory, however, came from the Italian Piero Sraffa (1898–1983), whom Keynes invited to the University of Cambridge. Commissioned by the Royal Economic Society, Sraffa edited the *The Works and Correspondence of David Ricardo* (1951–1973) and, in his own *Production of Commodities by Means of Commodities* (1960), reformulated the "standpoint of the old classical economists from Adam Smith to Ricardo" in a logically coherent form. He showed that, for a given system of production and a given wage rate, relative prices, profit rates, and rents can be consistently determined—without any recourse to supply and demand functions (see also chap. 12). People working in the Sraffian tradition are frequently dubbed "neo-Ricardians" (see chap. 12).

3
MARX AND THE SOCIALISTS

Socialist ideas, especially the call to introduce common property, have their roots in early Christianity. In his *Utopia* (1516), the English statesman and humanist Thomas More (1478–1535) developed the idea of a kind of communist society upon such Christian roots. But it was not until the emergence of the "social question" in the first half of the nineteenth century—in the wake of the Industrial Revolution—that socialist ideas really gained influence. Mention should be made of "early" and "utopian" socialists such as Henri de Saint-Simon (1760–1825), Charles Fourier (1772–1837), and Pierre-Joseph Proudhon (1809–1865) in France; the Welsh Robert Owen (1771–1858); and the German Johann Karl Rodbertus (1805–1875). Most were social reformers, who initiated and supported cooperative movements, founded experimental colonies (such as Owen's New Harmony on the banks of Indiana's Wabash River), and exerted some influence on the formation of institutions and legislation in several countries. There were also a number of marginalist economists who sympathized with certain socialist ideas; some advocated the socialization of land (like Gossen and Léon Walras; see chap. 4). The American economist and politician Henry George (1839–1897) in his 1879 book *Progress and Poverty* also called for a transformation of the land into collective property, on the ground that the rent collected on it belongs to all citizens and not only to the land's proprietors.

However, the most important socialist author by far is undoubtedly Karl Marx, backed by his friend and intellectual sparring partner Friedrich Engels (1820–1895). To his contribution we now turn.

KARL MARX Engels called Marx the founder of "scientific socialism," since Marx is said to have demonstrated the inevitability of socialism. Marx is credited with having unraveled the "law of motion" of capitalism. As Marx wrote in *Capital*: "Development of the productive forces of social labor is the historical task and justification of capital. This is just the way in which it unconsciously creates the material requirements of a higher mode of production"—of socialism. At the same time, as Marx sees it, the general rate of profits—the key variable of the capitalist system—has a tendency to fall, necessitating that capitalism give way to socialism. The "relations of production"—by this Marx means the property relations and especially the conflict between capital and labor—come into contradiction with the further development of the productive forces. At that point, capitalism has done its duty and has to go.

Close scrutiny shows that Marx's vision is a variation on the theme of the unintended consequences of human action—another kind of "invisible hand" argument, we might say. As capitalists tirelessly seek to increase their profits, they trigger a process they never intended or foresaw. Their specific individual rationality engenders effects that undermine their collective position and sweep away the capitalist society. "Behind their backs" the self-defeating forces set in motion by their aspirations gradually gain dominance. Marx apparently counted upon a ruse of history: precisely by squeezing ever-larger profits out of the mode of production they dominate, capitalists unintentionally facilitate the emergence of a classless society in which man's exploitation of his fellow man comes to an end.

Marx never succeeded in finishing his main work, *Capital: A Critique of Political Economy*. Only volume 1, *The Process of Production of Capital* (1867), was published during his lifetime; volumes 2 (1885) and 3 (1894) were posthumously published by Engels out of Marx's literary estate. As we now know, thanks to the Marx/Engels Collected Works (the so-called MEGA), Marx felt that his studies had not yet reached the degree of maturity necessary for publication, and he also began to have doubts about certain views he held. Most important perhaps, there was new evidence available that forced him to rethink his doctrine. While he had long seen Britain as the leading example of capitalism and its governing law of development, his attention was increasingly drawn to the United States, for which the statistical material was a great deal better, and whose dynamism showed no sign of slowing down.

MARX AND ENGELS ON THE UNITED STATES As contributors of a number of lead articles to the *New York Tribune*, commenting, among other things, on slavery, the financial and economic crisis of 1857, the Civil War, and the rise of joint-stock companies in the United States, Marx and Engels watched carefully what was going on in the New World. They were impressed by the rapid industrialization of the United States, which took place within a few decades in the mid-nineteenth century, and its rise to a world economic, political, and military power. The United States was an impressive example of what unfettered capitalism could bring about in a short period of time: it developed the productive powers "as in a greenhouse," as Marx wrote. At the same time the American form of capitalism differed markedly from the European one. In particular, it developed in parallel with political freedom extending to ever-larger segments of society and a comparatively high degree of social mobility. Unlike the European nations, and especially Britain, Prussia, and Russia, the United States was not under the spell of the remnants of a feudalist past. Therefore, the characteristic features of capitalism could be more clearly seen, because they were not contaminated by feudal elements.

The United States was able to make a fresh start, whereas Europe suffered from the yoke of history and tradition. Marx and Engels paid special attention to slavery in the United States, which found no parallel in contemporary Europe; according to them, slavery was a necessary part of early North American capitalism and crucial to the prosperity of the cotton industry. Without slavery, they said, the U.S. economy would not have developed as rapidly as it did: the blood, sweat, and tears of the slaves fueled its rise. However, as the Civil War documented, they saw slavery as having exhausted its role as a progressive element in U.S. capitalism. The developments in the United States and the way they differed from those in Europe are likely a deeper reason why Marx's completion of his magnum opus eluded him.

We now turn to the categories Marx used to analyze capitalism and its law of motion.

THEORY OF VALUE AND SURPLUS VALUE When two commodities are exchanged for one another at a certain ratio, Marx insisted, they must be equal in some dimension. The "common third" of both commodities, according to him, is nothing other than their shared characteristic as products of abstract human labor. The value of a commodity, accordingly, is determined by the amount of labor required for its production. Commodities, then, are exchanged according to the amounts of abstract labor embodied in them. At first sight this argument looks compelling—but does it hold up?

If, as Smith and Ricardo had argued, there are products such as wheat that may be said to go into making every product (either directly or indirectly), then these products would also be "common thirds." Hence we would have as many additional dimensions in which commodities could be said to be equal to one another as there are commodities entering as inputs (directly or indirectly) into all commodities.

But let us look further into this. The value of a commodity is equal to the "living" labor expended on it at the last stage of its production and the "dead" labor contained in the means of production used up to bring it forth, termed "constant capital" by Marx. In capitalism, human labor power becomes a commodity, and like other commodities, its value is equal to the value of the commodities required for its reproduction. If a worker labors nine hours a day, then he creates value in this amount. If his daily wage is just enough for him to purchase a daily ration of means of subsistence, and if a total of five hours has been expended in the production of this ration, then the five hours are what Marx called "variable capital" (the capital spent on labor) and the remaining four hours the "surplus value" created by the worker working for a day. This surplus value is pocketed by the capitalist when he sells the product of a day's work.

Marx calls the share of capital used for the purchase of labor power "variable capital" because "it both reproduces the equivalent of its own value, and also produces an excess, a surplus-value." If, in the course of the laborer's nine-hour day of work, means of production that are worth twenty hours are used up or productively consumed, then the value of the day's output amounts to 29 hours. The rate of profit attained is equal to the surplus value (4 hours) applied to the total capital advanced (the worker's wage representing a value of 5 hours and the constant capital of 20 hours, for a total of 25 hours) and so amounts, in this example, to 4/25 or 16 percent.

Marx calls the ratio of surplus value to variable capital the "rate of surplus value." At equal length and intensity of the workday, it tends to be uniform across all branches of the economy. Not so the "organic composition of capital"—the ratio of dead to living labor. For technical reasons, this varies between different branches of the economy. In a barber's shop, for example, the organic composition will be small, whereas in a nuclear power plant (run, as it is, using many other means of production) it will be large. But since surplus value is created in proportion to the variable capital (the wages) deployed and not in proportion to total capital (variable plus constant capital) deployed, the following problem arises: if commodities are exchanged at labor values, then branches with a higher organic composition of capital would attain a smaller rate of profit than those with a lower organic composition. But this, Marx insisted, is incompatible with competition, which tends to bring about an equalization of profit rates. Commodities could not, accordingly, be exchanged at labor values.

Contrary to the critique leveled at him by Eugen von Böhm-Bawerk (1851–1914), Marx was completely aware of this problem. He therefore proposed recalculating values in terms of production prices that satisfy the criterion of a uniform rate of profits. Marx dealt with this so-called transformation problem in volume 3 of *Capital*. He operated on the assumption that the "law of value" (as described earlier) is valid at the level of the overall economy: the sum total of all hours worked during a year, that is, the labor value of the gross domestic product (call this P), equals the sum total of all constant capitals used up (call this C) plus the sum total of all variable capitals (call this V) plus the sum total of all surplus values created (call it S), that is: $P = C + V + S$. This reflects a kind of economic law of conservation of the labor performed in the economic system and its value-creating potential. Marx then assumed that the sum total of all profits attained during a year is equal to the sum total of all surplus values created (S), while the sum total of all production prices is equal to the sum total of all values (P). He therefore saw the general rate of profits, ρ, as determined by the ratio of S to constant capital C plus variable capital V: $\rho = S/(C + V)$.

In general, however, this idea does not stand up to scrutiny. Marx conceded that the price ratio of two commodities can, and typically will, deviate from the labor value ratio—but what applies to the ratio of single commodities also applies to the ratio of bundles of commodities. The profit rate, however, conceived in material terms, is nothing other than the ratio of the overall economy's surplus product to the overall economy's capital— that is, a ratio of two composite bundles of commodities. In general, there is no reason to presume that the ratio expressed in terms of competitive prices will not deviate from the ratio expressed in terms of labor values. Hence, Marx's idea of the transformation of labor values in prices of production cannot be sustained except in special cases (such as the purely hypothetical case in which the organic compositions of capital happen to be the same everywhere in the economy). His suggested determination of the general rate of profits and of prices of production thus provides at best an approximate solution to the problem.

LAW OF THE TENDENCY OF THE RATE OF PROFITS TO FALL

Marx considered this "law" to be the "most important law from the historical standpoint," because it captures the transience of the capitalist mode of production. Marx rejected Ricardo's explanation that the fall of the rate of profit was due to diminishing returns in agriculture and mockingly said that Ricardo "flees from economics to seek refuge in organic chemistry." For "the rate of profit does not fall because labor becomes less productive," countered Marx, "but because it becomes more productive." Marx claimed that it falls *in spite of* technological progress, whereas for Ricardo technological progress works against its fall! Should one then assume, conversely, that Marx believed the rate of profits will rise with falling productivity?

Marx set the bar very high. In order to survive in the competitive struggle with his "hostile brothers," the other capitalists, each capitalist has to accumulate capital and introduce new technologies that allow him to create new products or lower the production costs of familiar products. The values of the different commodities fall, and along with them their production prices: less and less labor is needed to produce the various commodities. Marx saw the dominant form of technological progress in capitalism to be characterized by an increase in the organic composition of capital: more and more physical plant and equipment (tools, machines, etc.) is employed per worker—the production process becomes ever more mechanized. As a consequence of this an "industrial reserve army of the unemployed" emerges as workers are replaced by machines. This reserve army holds the demands of workers in check and is the reason why (as previously assumed) the workday is longer than it has to be in order to reproduce the worker's means of subsistence. Only for this reason is there surplus value and profit. But technological progress means that relatively less and less surplus value is created as direct labor is saved in relation to constant capital. This means there is a fall in the *maximum* rate of profits that would result if wages were hypothetically set equal to zero. But a falling maximum rate of profits, Marx thought, increasingly narrows the leeway for the actual rate of profits, until it finally forces this to fall as well.

Is Marx's reasoning convincing? Assume first that he was right in assuming that in capitalism the organic composition would always tend to increase and the maximum rate of profits therefore would always tend to fall. Obviously this is not the same thing as assuming that the organic composition will tend to infinity over time and the maximum rate of profits correspondingly to zero. If, however, the maximum rate of profits fell only to a lower boundary that is positive, the actual rate of profits need not fall over time. And is there even reason to presume that the organic composition will always tend to increase? Clearly, capitalists introduce new methods of production and thus technical progress because these increase labor productivity. But an increase in labor productivity cheapens the elements of variable capital (the means of subsistence for workers) and those of constant capital (the means of production): less and less labor is needed to produce the different kinds of commodities. For a given real wage, this implies that the variable capital needed to employ a worker for a day gets smaller and smaller. For a given length of the workday, surplus value therefore necessarily increases (and with it the rate of surplus value). The "cheapening" of the elements of constant capital, on the other hand, means that the value of constant capital will not increase, if at all, as fast as the increase of its physical volume suggests. Hence, given Marx's premises, S tends to increase, V tends to fall, and with regard to C we cannot say anything definite. What does this imply for the movement of $S/(C + V)$ over time? Not much. One might even be inclined to think that for a given real wage rate the rate of profits can be expected to rise.

Marx did not, at any rate, succeed in providing a conclusive proof of the "law" of the falling rate of profits. Ricardo had argued, like Marx, that a new method of production will only be adopted by cost-minimizing capitalists if it reduces costs of production per unit of output. However, unlike Marx, he had insisted that at a given and constant real wage, this implies that rather than falling, the general rate of profits will rise or remain constant. The rate of profits rises if the new method cheapens (directly or indirectly) the production of wage goods; it remains constant if the new method affects only other products ("luxuries"). Ricardo's view was shown conclusively to be correct, corroborated in the middle of the last century by Paul A. Samuelson, Piero Sraffa, and Nobuo Okishio (1927–2003).

SIMPLE AND EXTENDED REPRODUCTION In volume 2 of *Capital*, picking up on Quesnay's *Tableau économique*, Marx studied the interdependence between the different producing sectors of the economy. For this purpose he elaborated on the models of simple and extended reproduction, dividing the economy into a sector producing means of production, a second sector producing wage goods, and a third producing luxury goods. He worked out the balancing conditions under which these sectors expand in step with each other and developed the first multisectoral model of economic growth.

The purpose of the model was twofold. First, it allowed him to probe into the difficult problem of the accumulation of capital and the expansion of the economic system. This he did first by setting aside technical progress, assuming constant organic compositions of capital in all sectors. This was only a preparatory step toward analyzing the case of capital accumulation in the presence of technical change, reflected in rising organic compositions. Different types and speeds of technical change in the different sectors rendered the coordination problem in the private-decentralized economy infinitely more difficult, and Marx was keen to lay bare the origins of potential coordination failures. Therefore, and this is the model's second purpose, it allowed him to study why reproduction can fail and crises occur. In Marx's view capitalism is a crisis-prone system, and he saw the theory of reproduction as key to an understanding of this fact.

Marx singled out essentially four (possibly interrelated) causes of crises. First, they may result from sectoral "disproportions"—an excess production of commodities in one sector and a deficient production in another sector. Second, they may be caused by an increase in the inequality of income distribution, leading to a lack of effective consumption demand owing to insufficient purchasing power among workers ("underconsumption"). Third, crises may be triggered by a fall in the general rate of profits, which curbs the incentive to accumulate capital. Finally, in an economy in which money and credit play important roles, there is always the possibility of liquidity being withdrawn from circulation because of diminished profit expectations. This causes sales to falter and a crisis ensues.

However, Marx insisted that "permanent crises do not exist"—the system activates forces from within that eventually lead back to a normal state of affairs. For example, when the rate of profits falls and capital accumulation decelerates, the crisis that results destroys parts of the capital stock of an economy and increases unemployment, which in turn exerts a downward pressure on wages. As a consequence, profitability will recover, though not necessarily to its previous level (if the falling trend in the rate of profits prevails). This is why in his discussion of the law of the tendency of the rate of profits to fall, Marx assumed normal conditions and put on one side "realization problems"—that is, problems of realizing profits because the commodities produced do not find large enough markets to absorb them at their prices of production.

ALIENATION AND COMMODITY FETISHISM In his *Economic and Philosophic Manuscripts of 1844*, the young Marx developed a theory of social alienation under capitalism and its sublation (Hegel's concept of *Aufhebung*) under communism. The theory was the outcome of his critical engagement with the work of Georg Wilhelm Friedrich Hegel (1770–1831), who is considered to be the main representative of German idealism and is still intensively discussed in philosophy, especially economic philosophy. Elements of Marx's early views reemerge in all his later works. Marx considered the institution of "private property," which is fundamental in capitalism, to be the source of an encompassing alienation: in capitalism man is alienated from the product of his work, from his work as activity, from his nature as a human being, and from other men as human beings.

Alienation characterizes social states in which people treat others as means to the fulfillment of their interests. The commodity the worker produces is not for him or her but for the capitalist, and even the latter is not interested in the commodity as such but only in the profit its sale yields. Social relations lack mutual recognition and appreciation of the people involved: each one assesses the other only in terms his or her usefulness for one's own interests. Under capitalism, Marx maintained, human beings develop a quasi-religious relationship to products and attribute imaginary and supernatural features to commodities, money, and capital, such as the notion that money and capital are themselves capable of generating interest and profit. The commodity form of products involves a network of unequal relations between human beings, but this is hidden by commodity fetishism. The exploitative character of the system is thus concealed. Commodity fetishism creates a false consciousness about things and misreads reality. According to Marx, the destruction of the false consciousness is an indispensable step toward man's self-liberation.

ON THE IMPACT OF MARX'S WORK The impact of Marx's works was enormous—in economics, philosophy, sociology, history, and beyond. It inspired and spurred legions of fervent admirers and close followers—as well as fierce critics and intransigent opponents. No other economist-philosopher has exerted a comparable influence on people's thinking. And his impact was not limited to the realm of ideas and concepts. Political movements took up his message and translated it into political demands and, after having come to power, actual policy. At the beginning of the twentieth century, frequently after revolutionary upheavals, "socialist" regimes were established—including, of course, the Soviet Union in 1922, after the czarist regime in Russia was swept away by the 1917 October Revolution. While Marx and Engels had written relatively little on the economics of socialism, socialist regimes nevertheless typically appealed to their authority. But Marx had elaborated an analysis of capitalism and not a handbook containing ready-to-use recipes to run a socialist economy. It is no surprise that Marx's scientific work, devoid of much practical help in centrally planning and organizing a state, was elevated to the status of a sort of socialist Magna Carta of untouchable truths to be used in internal political power games.

We cannot know, of course, how Marx, the scientist and humanist, would have reacted to these regimes, but he likely would have been no less

merciless in dissecting their economic foundations and structures and criticizing them than he was with capitalism. Marx would surely have found it
unbearable to be stylized as a saint on a pedestal with his writings treated
like the holy scriptures.

The literature on Marx's political economy is huge and many ideas and
concepts found in his works have been picked up and developed. Just a few
are touched on here.

Marx was convinced that early competitive capitalism would gradually
be replaced by forms of trustified and monopoly capitalism, due to the
trend toward the concentration and centralization of capital, with larger
capitals swallowing smaller ones. As he predicted, this trend did actually
occur with the rise of huge trusts and conglomerates, often in the legal form
of joint-stock companies. In conjunction with the falling rate of profits that
Marx and his followers regarded as inevitable, this led to the formation of
several theories that sought to demonstrate the supposedly imminent col-
lapse of capitalism.

Rosa Luxemburg (1871–1919) and Otto Bauer (1881–1938) (the latter
a leading exponent of Austro-Marxism) conceived of imperialism as the
final stage of capitalism. After opportunities for making profits at home
had been exploited, they argued, nation-states would form colonies in an
attempt to raise the rate of profits through access to cheap raw materials
and receptive markets. However, the course of territorial expansion set by
nation-states would heighten the danger of war. The expansionist drive of
capitalism inevitably results in tensions between nations, incites peoples
against peoples, and eventually culminates in wars. Conventional economics, typically decried as "bourgeois," was attacked for its inclination to view
the world through the lens of perfect competition—which serves apologetic aims by ignoring the economic power of each single firm.

Perhaps the most important contribution to the Marxist literature was
Rudolf Hilferding's *Finance Capital*, published in 1910 and in his time
dubbed the fourth volume of *Capital*. Hilferding (1877–1941) identified
characteristic features of modern capitalism as, in addition to the formation
of cartels and trusts, the ever-tighter dovetailing of banking and industrial
capital. The growing importance of finance capital rested on its role as cred-
itor and on the establishment of new firms ("promoter's profit") and the
issuance and acquisition of stocks in light of the rapidly growing number of

joint-stock companies. Because of their interlocking assets, banks were able to use a relatively small share of their own equity capital to control a much larger volume of overall capital. According to Hilferding, there was a trend in industry toward a general cartel, and in the banking sector toward a single or "central bank." There emerged what Marx had called "a new financial aristocracy, a new variety of parasites in the shape of promoters, speculators and simply nominal directors; a whole system of swindling and cheating by means of corporation promotion, stock issuance, and stock speculation. It is private production without the control of private property." These passages read like commentaries on the latest financial crisis. Finance capital and the industrial capital it controls seek protection under the umbrella of the state; their quest for safeguards results in "organized capitalism."

In 1942, the American economist Paul M. Sweezy (1910–2004) published *The Theory of Capitalist Development*, a succinct introduction to Marx's economics. He and Paul A. Baran (1910–1964) also authored *Monopoly Capital: An Essay on the American Economic and Social Order* (1966). The book focuses on the problem of "surplus absorption"—that is, the discrepancy in the U.S. economy between its potential to generate a surplus and its failure to actually realize it. Due to a lack of effective demand, which reflects a Keynesian argument (chap. 9), capitalism is said to suffer from a realization problem. The state has to intervene with huge public expenditures, leading to ever-increasing budget deficits in the service of stabilizing an inherently unstable economy and improving capital's profits. Baran and Sweezy attributed a particularly important role to the enormous expansion of the military budget in the United States and the rise of what they called the "military-industrial complex." As the Soviet Union became a world military power, the arms race between the two nations striving for world political hegemony began.

The American economist Richard M. Goodwin (1913–1996) elaborated a mathematical model of Marx's idea of capitalism as an economic system that (of necessity) develops cyclically—that is, it periodically goes through slumps followed by recoveries and booms. Goodwin's model is a variant of the predator-prey model known in biology, with capitalists analogous to predators and workers to prey. When the rate of profits is high and the real wage rate correspondingly low, capital accumulation and the growth of the demand for workers will be high. As a consequence, the rate of unemployment will fall, strengthening the bargaining power of workers and their trade unions, which will sooner or later result in a rise in wages and a fall in the rate of profits. This will decelerate accumulation and the growth of the demand for labor until wages fall and the rate of profits rises again, and so on. Goodwin's model thus generates endogenous fluctuations in economic activity and in incomes shares (the profit and the wage share).

The input-output analysis of Wassily Leontief (1906–1999), the Russian economist who taught in the United States, harked back to Quesnay's *Tableau économique* and Marx's reproduction schemes. It became an important instrument of empirical economic research for investigations looking into, for instance, the impact of economic policy measures on the size and sectoral composition of output, the employment effects of the introduction and diffusion of new production technologies, and the environmental effects of various tax systems.

4
THE RISE OF MARGINALISM

According to a widespread view, there was a "marginalist revolution" in the final third of the nineteenth century that led to a rejection of classical economics and a reorientation of the field. (Whether or not this truly was a "revolution" is discussed later.) The most influential marginalist thinkers were the Briton William Stanley Jevons (1835–1882), the Austrian Carl Menger (1840–1921), and the Frenchman Léon Walras (1834–1910). Alfred Marshall attempted a reconciliation of this new thinking with the old theories of the classical economists; instead of "political economy," Marshall talked of "economics." Eventually, the designations "neoclassical economics" and the "theory of supply and demand" took hold with regard to the new school of economic thought.

CHARACTERISTICS OF MARGINALIST THINKING In spite of many differences in detail, the new theories displayed some remarkable points of agreement. I single out eight defining characteristics of marginalist thinking, and compare these with classical thinking to show how they differ.

First was a new definition of the field and the characters that populate it. According to the Briton Lionel Robbins (1898–1984), economics studies "human behavior as a relationship between ends and scarce means which have alternative uses" (1932). It conceives of humans as optimizing entities: minimizing costs and maximizing profits (in the case of firms) or maximizing utility (in the case of consumers or households). And *homo economicus* conquered the arena on which this new theoretical orientation was staged. While David Hume had maintained that man is "but a heap of contradictions" and reason "the slave of the passions," marginalist economic thought became preoccupied with simple, linear characters who know what they want and efficiently pursue it within the means available to them.

While the classical authors had started their analyses with a view to society as a whole as they saw it before their eyes, stratified in different classes, the marginalists began their analysis from the single needy individual. They put to themselves the task of reconstructing society from individuals, described in abstract terms (their needs and wants and capabilities and their interaction in interdependent markets). Hence, society and the economy were the result rather than the starting point of the enterprise. Joseph A. Schumpeter called this approach to economic phenomena "methodological individualism." As his Austrian peer Carl Menger had insisted, beginning the analysis with an investigation of the needs, wants, and space of possibilities of a Robinson Crusoe on his island defined the appropriate perspective on economic matters, because it allowed one to analyze the economic behavior of the individual as if in a vacuum. In a next step, individuals were seen to engage in social and economic interactions only if and to the extent to which it served their self-interest. Social and economic relations were thus telescoped back to single agents.

Second, it is sometimes said that marginalist economics advocates a purely subjectivist theory of value and distribution, in contrast with the objectivist theory of classical economics. Austrian economists like Carl Menger and Ludwig von Mises (1881–1973) did indeed advance the thesis that all value (and cost) is ultimately derived exclusively from the subjective evaluations of individuals. However, this view was not shared among all marginalist thinkers. Rather, it was Alfred Marshall's interpretation that prevailed, which contended that a complete theory of prices and income distribution must take into account both objective and subjective factors or "forces"—that of supply and that of demand. In his attempt to present his own theory as a continuation of and elaboration on the classical one, Marshall maintained that classical theory was essentially limited to an analysis of the production and supply side, whereas the demand side was still in its infancy. What was needed to complement the classical theory was a theory of consumption and demand—a task Marshall prided himself on having accomplished.

A few observations are apposite on this. First, as we have seen, Smith and his fellow classicists determined the rate of profits and relative prices in terms of a given system of production and a given real wage. A logically coherent formulation of the classical approach shows that no other data, such as demand functions, are needed to accomplish the task. But while their explanation of the rate of profits and prices differed from the margin-alist one, it was not— as Marshall and other marginalist authors believed— incomplete or indeterminate. Since a given system of production involves given output levels, the classical determination took into account social effectual demands of the different commodities. Marshall's classification of his own theory as firmly entrenched in the classical tradition was therefore dubious. From a promotional point of view it had, of course, the enormous advantage of presenting the new theory as being erected on the shoulders of the sung heroes of the discipline such as Adam Smith or David Ricardo.

So what was the difference, then, between the two schools as regards the demand side? In the dynamic perspective of classical economics, new or improved qualities of known goods are constantly made avail-able, forcing learning processes among consumers as the range of goods gets broader. Initially, this only affects the well-to-do, but eventually it also reaches the lower strata of society. The former try to distinguish themselves from the latter, while the latter try to imitate the former. This behavior fuels the dynamics of consumption and is a veritable incentive to product innovation. At some stage of economic development, for exam-ple, only the rich will be able to afford the equipment needed to play ten-nis. With rising levels of income, the lower strata of society, in an effort to imitate the rich, will start playing tennis themselves. To keep apart from the "plebs," the rich are bound to turn to golf, later to sailing or polo, and so on. Accordingly, in the classical view, there are no isolated and autono-mous individuals whose consumption behavior can be described abstractly as a confrontation of the agent with a given world of goods: man is a social animal who cares about what others do, imitating them or distancing him-self from them, as the case may be. Yet in the static perspective of marginal-ism, it is precisely the consumption behavior of an isolated individual that is the focus of interest for the economist. (Interestingly, as we will see in chap. 10, the Robinson Crusoe–type character lives on in much of modern macroeconomics in the assumption that there is a single "representative agent.") The marginalist concept of given preferences, depicted in a utility function (defined in terms of a given and constant set of goods), also does not provide for the emergence of new goods and hence has no way of dealing with dynamic cases. It therefore should not come as a surprise that with marginalism attention initially shifted away from questions about development and economic growth to questions about the allocation of resources toward alternative uses.

The difference between the two approaches can be illustrated by means of the famous water-and-diamond paradox Adam Smith posited. He drew the attention to the fact that while water, which is indispensable for man to survive and thus has a very high use value, is typically very inexpensive on the English isle, diamonds, whose use value is negligible, are very expensive. Menger and others later accused Smith of failing to convincingly resolve the paradox, because he lacked the theory of marginal utility. While it is true that Smith had no such theory, the criticism is difficult to sustain. Smith argued that water is cheap because its costs of attainment are small, whereas diamonds are dear because the costs of finding and working them are high. But why do people wish to acquire diamonds? Smith was clear that to answer this question, one must realize that this is not a simple subject-object relation—the individual and the diamond. Rather, the main (albeit not the only) reason why diamonds are wanted is because they allow individuals to signal their riches and status to others. The more expensive a diamond is, the better it is suited to perform this function, because others cannot afford it. In order to understand the consumption behavior of even a single individual one typically has to know the individual's position in the social pyramid. Robinson Crusoe likely had little interest in diamonds, if you follow Smith's thinking, because he lacked other people to impress.

Third, the focus of attention shifted to activity taking place "at the margin"—thus the name: marginalism. The analysis advocated by this school revolves around a very particular type of counterfactual reasoning, leading to questions of the following kind: By how much *would* output increase (or decrease), if a firm (or the economy as a whole) had a little more (or less) of some productive factor at its disposal and the same quantities of all the other factors? By how much *would* the utility of an individual be increased (or reduced), if he or she consumed a little more (or less) of one of the consumption goods and the same quantities of all the other goods? Hence the attention focused on a comparison between a given situation and a hypothetical alternative situation. The alternative situation was constructed by the theorist, who was thus no longer the detached observer of the economic system under consideration, as the classical economist had been. Rather, he was an experimenter who contemplated the effects of hypothetical perturbations of the system. Whereas the classical economists sought to analyze the economic system as it existed, the marginalist economists sought to understand its properties by confronting it with a constructed system that was assumed to be adjacent to the actual system.

This methodological divide is of great importance and accounts for deep differences between the classical and marginalist approaches and the results they obtain in various fields of economic inquiry. It is only with marginalism that the twin concepts of "marginal productivity" and "marginal utility" entered the intellectual arena, and along with these the mathematical tools of differential and integral calculus became a part of economics. The German estate owner and agrarian innovator Johann Heinrich von Thünen (1783–1850) was one of the first to propagate the marginal method with regard to production, while the Germans Karl Heinrich Rau (1782–1870) and Hermann Heinrich Gossen (1810–1858) pioneered its application to the sphere of consumption.

Fourth, the marginalists conceived of the production side and the consumption side in almost complete analogy with each other, with similar laws prevailing in both spheres. The leading idea here was derived from the classical principle of intensively diminishing returns. If more and more labor is employed on a given piece of land, then from a certain point onward every incremental unit of labor will bring about an ever-smaller increase in output, until the increase becomes equal to zero (and then negative). That is to say, the marginal productivity of labor declines as more and more labor is employed on the piece of land. Marginalism adopted this principle and generalized it indiscriminately to *all* factors of production as well as to the sphere of consumption. If an economic agent consumes more and more of a good, then the agent's total utility rises but marginal utility falls: each additional unit of the good brings about an ever-smaller increase in utility, until the increase becomes equal to zero (and thereafter negative). There is thus an analogy between a given piece of land on which more and more labor is employed and a needy human being who consumes more and more of a good. Just as labor on a given plot of land creates output, though at a diminishing marginal productivity, a good consumed by a given individual creates utility, though at a diminishing marginal utility.

The marginal productivity principle formed the basis for the marginalists' explanation of income distribution. The factors of production, they maintained, will in competitive conditions be paid according to their marginal productivities, because if a factor was paid less (or more) it would be profitable to increase (or decrease) its employment. In this perspective, the real wage rate reflects the marginal productivity of labor, while the rate of profits reflects the marginal productivity of capital. However, as we will see in chapter 12, this explanation of income distribution ran into serious difficulties, first recognized by the Swedish economist Knut Wicksell (1851–1926).

Fifth, the marginalists understood all economic problems as "constrained optimization problems." The available technological knowledge and available productive resources were the constraints on production, while household income and commodity prices were the constraints on consumption. Marginalism proceeded from a different constellation of data than did classical economics in tackling the problems of value and distribution. It assumed as given: (1) the technological alternatives of production, (2) the preferences of agents, (3) the economy's initial endowment with productive resources of all kinds (labor, land, capital goods etc.), and (4) the distribution of property rights to this endowment among the members of society. By way of these data, the prices and the quantities produced of the various goods, the rates of remuneration of the different factors of production (wages, profits and rents), and the employment of the factors in the different sectors of the economy were determined. It deserves to be stressed that the marginalists understood *all* prices as indicators of the relative scarcities of the various goods or factors. They also treated reproducible goods (especially capital goods) in terms of scarcity and thus rent theory—unlike in classical economics, where this was only the case with respect to scarce natural resources. The marginalist argument therefore presupposes situations in which there is the full employment of all factors of production. If there is not full employment of labor, for example, workers are assumed to bid down the wage rate until there is full employ-ment. If however, the market-clearing wage rate happens to be smaller than the subsistence rate—or if there is no level of the wage rate that clears the market—the survival of the system would be in jeopardy. Say's law was thus taken to apply in a comprehensive sense that also included the labor market. Marginalist attention henceforth focused on equilibria of microunits (firms and households) and of the economic system as a whole. Agents in equilibrium have no reason to reorient themselves, since they are already optimally utilizing all the opportunities available to them. Without much further ado equilibria were assumed to be stable—that is, deviations from equilibria would activate forces from within the system to correct the deviation.

Sixth, it was with the marginalists that the ceteris paribus assumption became prominent in economics and in some areas even assumed center stage. We have already drawn attention to the specific kind of counterfac-tual reasoning involved. The "effects" resulting from hypothetical changes in endowments, preferences, and so on were captured by comparing the pre- and the postchange equilibrium. The marginalist method of analysis was thus comparative statics, not dynamics. It was assumed that the change would instantaneously lead to the new equilibrium. The path by which this was supposed to happen was not investigated, as this was considered to be too difficult. Assume, for example, that the population of an economy increases by 10 percent, all other things being equal. If this happened in a real economic system, it would in all probability profoundly upset the original equilibrium (provided there was one) and induce an avalanche of adjustment processes. Marginalist theory cuts the story short and assumes there will be a new equilibrium, whose properties can be known indepen-dently of the processes by which it is attained.

In adopting the marginal method of hypothetical changes it was not always clear what was meant by the isolated change of the available amount of a given factor of production. The lack of clarity concerned especially the factor "capital." If, realistically, several types of capital goods are employed (machines, conveyor belts, computers, etc.), then what is meant by an increase or decrease in the "amount of capital"? Does it mean that there will be proportionally more of each and every type of capital good? And if it does, can it be assumed that all these capital goods will be needed fully in the new equilibrium, given the amounts of the other factors? Or will some be partially or totally superfluous? And could one in this case speak of an "equilibrium"? These are difficult questions to answer and I cannot go into details here. It must suffice to report the conclusion Knut Wicksell drew from this. He concluded that a unified treatment of physical capital in terms of this approach is only possible if one treats the amount of capital as a value sum, whose material composition is an unknown and is ascertained only as part and parcel of the equilibrium solution. This is not a very satisfactory procedure, according to Wicksell, because it is far from clear what an initial endowment of a certain sum of value, designed to represent the quantity of capital in the economy, means in production, where only physical capital goods (ploughs, tractors, blast furnaces, etc.) matter.

Seventh, both in production and in consumption, marginalists emphasized the possibility of substitution: a given level of production or utility can be achieved with different combinations of factors or consumption goods. According to Marshall the principle of substitution is one of the most important principles in economics. Factors and goods are seen to be interchangeable to a certain degree. This was significant for intellectual experiments that considered how a consumer, a firm, or an economic system as a whole would respond to changing conditions. Take, for example, the case of a consumer who enjoys eating both apples and pears. Assume now that the price of apples doubles ceteris paribus. How will the consumer respond to this? He or she might reduce his or her consumption of apples and increase that of pears and thus substitute the good whose price has stayed constant for the now relatively more expensive one. In a more comprehensive perspective this gives rise to additional effects: factors could be withdrawn from producing apples and channeled into producing pears, thus changing the levels of outputs and the allocation of factors of production, and so on.

The theory of "general equilibrium" is devoted to discussing all these effects. The theory assumes that all responses of agents (producers and consumers) to market signals are known: that is, any learning processes that might happen en route (and thus change the responses and with them the equilibrium toward which the system is supposed to move) are put to one side. In other words, the general equilibrium theorists treat agents as "open secrets," so to speak. When talking about the effects of some change, we typically consider only the primary effects and occasionally the secondary ones; this theory seeks to take into consideration all effects, direct and indirect. The results it obtains therefore typically differ from what one might have expected when focusing attention only on first-round effects. In particular, income effects cannot generally be ruled out. Income distribution will typically change, and with different income recipients having different preferences, demand will change too. A higher price of apples, for example, will benefit apple producers, whose profits will now be increased relative to those of pear producers. This will attract capital in search of the best remuneration, and so on.

The basic idea here was not new: looking at the system as a whole, the marginalists insisted that the constraint binding changes in prices and the distributive variables be respected. For example, a rise (or fall) in the real wage rate always affects other distributive variables, relative prices, and so on. And in an economy in which all factors of production are fully employed, increasing the output of one commodity will typically necessitate a reduction in the output level of at least one other commodity.

As Ricardo already knew well, a rise (or fall) in the real wage rate leads inevitably to a reduction (an increase) in the rate of profits, given the system of production in use.

Eighth, one particularly restrictive use of the ceteris paribus assumption became prominent in marginalism: the case in which only a single market is examined and interdependencies with all other markets are put on one side. This is the method of "partial equilibrium" championed by Alfred Marshall. Its characteristic feature is that it ignores the constraint binding changes of the different magnitudes mentioned earlier. Its prominence even in contemporary economics must not distract attention from its problematic character. Marshall was aware of the highly restrictive conditions under which the partial equilibrium method could be applied (see chap. 5) and insisted that propositions acquired through partial analysis and the economic policy conclusions based thereon should be treated with the utmost caution. However, his warnings have been and still are widely ignored in large parts of the profession. This is why the graph typically used in partial equilibrium analysis has sadly come to represent the very badge of economics: intersecting supply and demand curves, also known as the "Marshallian cross." We will see later what is problematic about them.

The analytical workhorse of much of marginalist theory is the case of "perfect competition": numerous (in the extreme: infinitely many) fully informed suppliers face numerous (in the extreme: infinitely many) fully informed demanders. None of the agents wields economic power. Of course, every real society is permeated by power and information asymmetries—a fact that Adam Smith, among others, threw into sharp relief.

Given all this—does it make sense to speak of a "marginalist revolution"? Yes and no. No, because the concepts of marginal productivity and marginal utility had been known for a long time. Yes, because an entirely new explanation of income distribution was presented that sought to explain *all* rates of remuneration (wage rate, profit rate, land rent) in terms of a *single* principle—the principle of marginal productivity with respect to each respective factor (labor, capital, land). The explanation under consideration conceives of all incomes as indexes of relative scarcities of the respective factor services. This presupposes that all factors are fully employed. Marginal productivity theory and Say's law thus turn out to be Siamese twins. In classical theory, by contrast, only land rent is considered as reflecting the scarcity of a particular quality of land, while profit is explained in terms of surplus theory. Capital goods, unlike land, can be produced and reproduced and therefore can be scarce only in the short run.

FORERUNNERS: THÜNEN, COURNOT, AND RAU The concept of marginal productivity was first developed by the German economist Johann Heinrich von Thünen in 1850 in the second of the three volumes of *The Isolated State*. He attempted to verify the concept empirically on his landed estate, by cultivating adjacent plots of land with different intensities (that is, by employing different amounts of labor per hectare) and then comparing the results. Thünen is also known for his formula for the "natural wage" that adorns his gravestone, $\sqrt{ap}$, with a as the subsistence wage and p as the productivity of labor. As early as the first volume of his treatise in 1826, Thünen established the general condition for maximizing profit in a firm: for a given quantity brought to market, it must hold that marginal costs (the costs of the last unit produced) equal marginal revenue (the revenue increase resulting from the sale of this unit). (On Thünen's pathbreaking contributions to spatial economics, see chap. 12.)

The concept of the demand curve for a good, expressing the dependence of the demand for a good on the good's price, was first introduced in 1838 by the French mathematician Antoine-Augustin Cournot (1801–1877) and independently of him shortly afterward by the German Karl Heinrich Rau (1792–1870). Rau may also be said to have been the first to introduce in substance (not verbatim) the concept of marginal utility. Cournot deserves credit for having treated the case of monopoly and confirmed the aforementioned condition for profit maximization (marginal revenue = marginal cost).

FORERUNNER: HERMANN HEINRICH GOSSEN The only work Gossen ever published, *The Laws of Human Relations and the Rules of Human Action Derived Therefrom* (1854), remained totally unnoticed for a quarter of a century. And yet it contained a formulation of marginal utility theory, inspired by Rau, that was well ahead of its time. Gossen is therefore rightly seen as one of the pioneers of the theory.

Gossen believed he had revealed "the real purpose of man's life, willed by his Creator" and saw himself as the Copernicus or Newton of economics. Since the Creator has undertaken "calculations," according to Gossen, mathematics is also required to decipher the plan of Creation. The denunciation of pleasure promoted by the Christian churches is based on a misunderstanding, insisted Gossen. Not mortification was given unto man, but rather maximizing the "sum of life's pleasures"—unadulterated hedonism.

Gossen based his argument on two premises. The first: "The magnitude (intensity) of pleasure decreases continuously if we continue to satisfy one and the same enjoyment without interruption until satiety is ultimately reached." This factual assertion of decreasing marginal utility is known as Gossen's first law. The second: "In order to maximize his total pleasure, an individual free to choose between several pleasures but whose time is not sufficient to enjoy all to satiety must . . . satisfy first all pleasures in part in such a manner that the magnitude (intensity) of each single pleasure at the moment when its enjoyment is broken off shall be the same for all pleasures." The maxim advanced here is known as Gossen's second law.

Most accounts of Gossen's work overlook his emphasis on the allocation of scarce time for alternative activities. An example can help illustrate this. Start with the assumption that twelve hours in each twenty-four-hour day are used for sleeping and personal hygiene. For simplicity's sake, let us say that for the remaining twelve hours there are only two kinds of available pleasures that (for the sake of argument!) cannot occur simultaneously: watching movies or eating spaghetti. A movie takes two hours, consuming a portion of spaghetti half an hour. As Ian Steedman put it: *Consumption takes time!* So our individual can watch six movies or eat twenty-four portions of spaghetti, or arrange for some combination of the two pleasures. The maxim to follow now becomes: break off your activities exactly at the moment when the increase in utility of both (at the last second before stopping) is exactly the same. How many portions of spaghetti a particular individual will optimally eat and how many movies he or she will optimally watch depends, of course, on the individual's preferences; different individuals may exhibit different consumption optima. Even in the land of milk and honey, owing to the time-robbing nature of consumption, there will always be an optimization problem in need of resolution.

All human beings are subject to the time constraint, and many also to an income constraint. Gossen's argument helps explain one finding of happiness research: with rising family income comes the subjective perception of an increase in happiness, but only up to a point; thereafter happiness tends to stagnate. Ever-higher incomes do not make people happier. While one could afford more goods, one lacks the time to enjoy them.

How is individual egoism related to the welfare of society, according to Gossen? He is naively optimistic: the brake on consumption that we owe to time constraints curbs greed and cravings. And owing to the productivity-increasing effects of the division of labor and the gains from trade emphasized by Smith, people cooperate and so become dependent on one another. The result of both is that each individual in pursuit of "his own personal welfare" simultaneously contributes to the "welfare of all mankind." An all-powerful and all-benevolent superior being created the world and its inhabitants in such a way that "there is nothing further wanting in the world to make it a perfect paradise."

Alas, Gossen's glad tidings of joy at first fell flat—during his lifetime, only ten copies of his book were sold. When the prophet of hedonism died at a fairly young age, he was filled with bitterness.

WILLIAM STANLEY JEVONS Jevons gained considerable attention with his book *The Coal Question* (1865). In it, he painted a dismal picture of England's further development. The exploitation of coal deposits, he contended, supported a pessimistic outlook on the world, similar to Malthus's. Yet, while in Malthus it was the scarcity of an assumedly inexhaustible resource (land) that spelled trouble for people, now it was the petering out of an exhaustible resource (coal). With the benefit of hindsight we may say that both authors underestimated the importance of technological progress and alternative energy sources. Jevons's work can be viewed as a forerunner of the Club of Rome study about *The Limits to Growth* (1972) and as an early contribution to resource and energy economics.

However, lasting fame came to Jevons with another book: his *Theory of Political Economy* (1871). In that work he advocated a break with classical economics, which he alleged was based on "mazy and preposterous" assumptions. He also insisted that to qualify as a respectable science, economics should look to physics and use mathematics. Jevons's mathematical talents were actually quite modest, but his appeal was extremely successful.

His main attack was against the classical theory of value: the value of a commodity, he argued, is not determined by the amount of labor it requires but by its *"final degree of utility"*—Jevons's term for marginal utility. This, however, is subjective—it is decided by each individual consumer and reflects his or her needs and wants. Although Jevons did have an equivalent to Gossen's first law, he had no counterpart to the second law. Like Gossen, he assumed that the marginal utility of a good is dependent on that good only and not also on the amount of other goods consumed. The temporal dimension of consumption, which had assumed center stage in Gossen, played no role in Jevons's analysis.

Although Jevons accentuated the demand side and advocated an anticlassical program, close scrutiny shows that his argument remained stuck in first gear. This can best be seen by the fact that Jevons saw relative prices in equilibrium to be equal to relative labor costs. What was novel in his thinking was not any rejection of the labor theory of value but rather a new causality: proceeding from marginal utility, this causality ended with labor. In his view this implied putting the causality of the classical authors, who had started from labor, upside down. Jevons argued as follows: demand, based on the marginal utility principle, determines the composition of output.

In equilibrium the supply of goods is equal to the demand for goods, where the supply of goods is effectuated by the expenditure of labor. In equilibrium the "law of cost" applies, which means that the (labor) costs of production are equal to the prices of goods. Hence the labor theory of value, which had been thrown out the front door entered the house again by the back door.

Interestingly, other economists like the Austrian Eugen von Böhm-Bawerk and the American John Bates Clark (1847–1938) came to the same conclusion and insisted that the law of cost amounted to the same thing as the labor theory of value. Now this may seem to imply that they reverted to where economics was at the time of Smith and Ricardo, whose doctrines were frequently identified with the labor theory of value. But ironically, as we saw in chapter 2, none of the classical authors actually advocated the theory ascribed to them. That is, none of them maintained that relative prices were strictly proportional to relative labor quantities needed in their production. Smith and especially Ricardo were fully aware of the fact that compound interest had an influence on relative prices and the role the time profiles of labor expenditures played in this. We are thus confronted with the following perplexing situation: classical economics was rejected by some of its leading critics not least because of the labor theory of value, which none of the classical authors actually held, while none other than the critics advocated the view that relative prices are proportional to relative labor quantities. An irony indeed!

Jevons's work paved the way for the "temporal" or "Austrian" theory of capital and interest enunciated by Böhm-Bawerk in *Capital and Interest* (1884–1889), which Knut Wicksell developed further in *Value, Capital, and Rent* (1893). As the Austrian thinkers saw it, capital means first and foremost a smaller or larger quantum of means of subsistence for laborers. Such means of subsistence allow one to embark on more or less "roundabout" processes of production. That is to say, they permit an extension of the length of the "production period," which is the time calculated from the moment labor is first employed, across further stages involving the production of intermediary products, and lasting until the final product is completed. One can, for example, hunt for fish with bare hands, spear them using a previously sharpened stick, or catch them with a boat and net, and so on. Such extensions of the production period, Böhm-Bawerk contended, are "superior" in the sense that they yield a larger output per unit of labor employed—that is, they exhibit a larger labor productivity. The increase in output due to a lengthening of the period of production is one of the key ingredients of the Austrian explanation of a positive rate of interest (the term the Austrian economists used as a synonym for rate of profits) and the accumulation of capital. The other key ingredient is the concept of a positive "rate of time preference": an individual is assumed to prefer a given bundle of goods today to the same bundle in a week from now, and the latter to the same bundle in two weeks from now, and so on. In other words, individuals are impatient with respect to consumption. The implication is that they are only willing to overcome their impatience—that is, are willing to save—if the rate of interest on savings is larger than the individual rate of time preference. Saving, however, extends the period of production, which leads to a higher output per unit of subsistence bundle (which is needed to employ workers) invested. As long as the latter increment is larger than the rate of time preference, there will be savings.

CARL MENGER Carl Menger's *Principles of Economics*, the seminal work of the so-called Austrian school, was also published in 1871—the same year as Jevons's *Theory of Political Economy*. Menger dedicated the book to the German Wilhelm Roscher (1817–1894), a leading exponent of the older historical school, and picked up on earlier contributions from the German use value school and the school of Salamanca (see chap. 1). These early German economists emphasized the importance of people's attribution of value to things, their estimation of goods, for explaining the goods' prices. While according to Menger the contributions of these authors pointed in the right direction, what was still missing was a general theory of human economic behavior. This Menger sought to elaborate with the intention of putting economics on a solid basis.

Menger's reasoning is as follows. He started from the assumption that all goods can be brought into a hierarchical order, with the first order comprising goods that are directly able to satisfy needs and wants, the second order comprising goods needed in the production of goods of the first order, the third order comprising goods needed in the production of the goods of the second order, and so on. Menger subsumed under the concept of "goods" not only products but also labor and land services. Goods of higher order were also called "cost goods" by later Austrian economists. How did Menger see the values of the goods of various categories determined? According to the "causal-genetic" perspective he and his followers assumed, the preferences and estimations of the economic subjects—the consumers—directly determined the values of the "goods of first order." From these values, Menger was convinced, one could derive the values of all other goods, that is, "goods of higher order." But how, precisely?

Menger's explanation of values had to tackle what is known as the "imputation problem": How is the already determined value of a finished product divided up into the values of the factors of production that have contributed to its manufacture via the several stages involved? Menger tried to solve the problem in terms of what he called the "loss principle." He asked: By how much would the output of a good fall, if one unit of some input needed in its production was taken away? The ensuing loss in output multiplied by the predetermined value of the product was the value of the input under consideration. However, Menger's solution to the imputation problem cannot be sustained, not least because it involves multiple counting. An example may clarify the problem at hand. Assume that a truck is indispensable in the production of some good (say, a transport service), and assume now that one wheel is taken away from the truck. Then the product can no longer be produced, and following Menger's logic the value of the wheel ought to be equal to the value of the transport service. In this case no other input (for example, the driver's contribution) could have a positive value. What is more, the same argument applies to each of the remaining three wheels, which means that according to the loss principle the costs would be four times the value of the product.

Menger did not succeed in providing a satisfactory answer to the imputation problem, with whose solution stands or falls his approach to the problem of value. Friedrich von Wieser (1851–1926), to whom we owe the term "marginal utility" (*Grenznutzen*), took up the challenge and first pointed out further problems of the Austrian approach. He drew attention to the fact that in modern industrial systems production is a circular process in which products are produced by means of products. Even in agriculture, circularity cannot be ruled out: wheat is produced by means of wheat used as seed and livestock is produced by means of livestock used for breeding. Hence corn and many other products are goods belonging to different orders, a fact the theory has to respect. Further, what if the number of goods of first order is larger than the number of goods of all other orders? What if the number is smaller? In the first case the imputation problem would be overdetermined, while in the second case it would be underdetermined. Wieser emphasized that a solution to the imputation problem presupposes a system that contains just as many simultaneous "price = cost" equations as there are different cost goods or input factors whose prices need to be determined. In a circular framework the values of all goods have to be determined simultaneously. Menger's successivist approach cannot be sustained. The "causal-genetic" explanation is not good enough, and values cannot be ascertained without some mathematics.

There is also the following problem, to which Menger already drew attention. Before something can be consumed, it has to be produced. But how do producers know what and how much to produce? They need to form expectations about likely demands, which could prove to be wrong. Consumers can also be mistaken; they might erroneously hope to satisfy a need by consuming a particular good. Tellingly, "Time and Error" is the title of a subsection in Menger's *Principles*: all economic action takes place in time, and since one cannot know the future, uncertainty prevails. Expectations influence present decisions and by extension prices and quantities.

Starting from Menger's loss principle, Wieser elaborated what was later called the concept of "opportunity costs." For example, if a multiproduct firm constrained by given amounts of productive resources and a given technical knowledge wishes to produce more of a particular product, by how much must the firm reduce the output(s) of some other product(s)? The opportunity cost of producing one more unit of the first product is given by the amount of some other product whose production the firm has to forgo.

Menger's message fell on fertile ground with advocates of what became known as the radically subjectivist branch of the Austrian school. Its most influential spokesman was Ludwig von Mises, who, after teaching in Vienna and Geneva in 1940 immigrated to the United States, where he was appointed to an endowed chair at New York University in 1945. Mises was a steadfast libertarian, whose early work focused on the role of money and of the banking sector, which, by expanding money and credit circulation, was regarded to be responsible for inflation and business cycles. Money, he insisted, was not neutral with regard to the real side of the economy, was not a veil that only covered real affairs. Rather, it intervened in them and affected output, employment, allocation of resources, and so on. According to Mises, economics ought to be a doctrine "of human action and not of non-action as in the doctrine of equilibrium"—that is, the theory of the neoclassical mainstream, to which he was strictly opposed. He dubbed the doctrine he espoused "praxeology." Mises was also fiercely opposed to the use of mathematics in economics and the idea that economics should be shaped in the image of physics. He rejected the view that the quality of a theory ought to be decided in terms of how well it predicted the future. Socialism, Mises insisted, was logically impossible, because it was unable to solve the calculation problem and organize a complex society. His radical laissez-faire comes to the fore in his advocacy of a sort of "domino theory" according to which any state intervention in the economic system, because of the distortions it generates, is bound to lead to further interventions and eventually to socialism. His prediction did not come true.

Mises had several followers, especially in the United States, both in academia and in politics. It suffices to mention the economists Ludwig Lachmann (1906–1990), Murray Rothbard (1926–1995), and Israel M. Kirzner (b. 1930). Misesian ideas resonate, for example, in the writings of the Russian-American novelist Ayn Rand (1905–1982) and in proposals of members of the Tea Party.

THE *METHODENSTREIT* (BATTLE OVER METHODS) Underlying many of the discussions surrounding marginalism was the question of the appropriate method for economics. Menger played an important role in the *Methodenstreit* debate—the "battle over methods"—which was between adherents of the "historical-ethical" approach in Germany, led by Gustav Schmoller (1838–1917), and representatives of the marginal utility school that was growing in strength, as led by Menger. Before Schmoller, Wilhelm Roscher had advocated carrying out detailed empirical and historical research in addition to theoretical work: he held that inductive and deductive methods were equally indispensable. Schmoller's position, by contrast, was radical and often regarded not only as atheoretical but even as antitheoretical. His influence in Germany was considerable.

Schmoller's followers rejected the message of Menger's *Principles* and insisted that the formulation of an economic theory could only be the result of thorough historical studies and the discovery of regularities in behavior. This prompted Menger to attack historicism in a treatise published in 1883. He contended that social facts had to be derived by starting from the needy individual, and since any human being is in this regard in the same position, the theory must be developed by using observations and personal experiences: fundamental insights into economic behavior do not become possible only after a certain mass of historical facts have been collected but are possible here and now by introspection. The insights gained in this way must then be generalized, thus broadening their content, and used in analyzing social interactions. Schmoller responded, Menger countered; the debate widened and became sharper, personal, irreconcilable. Both sides took their respective positions to excess.

From today's perspective, the *Methodenstreit* was intellectually astonishingly sterile. In terms of university politics in Germany, however, it led the adherents of the historical school to close ranks and focus on keeping theoretical minds away from their departments. But in Austria economic theory flourished, with Böhm-Bawerk, Wieser, Friedrich August von Hayek (1899–1992), and Schumpeter the major agents of the upsurge. In Germany, by contrast, proponents of historicism—also known as *Kathedersozialisten* (socialists of the chair)—advised Bismarck on his social reform policy designed to curb the rise of the Social Democrats by improving the living conditions of the working class.

The so-called Freiburg school, or ordoliberalism, of Walter Eucken (1891–1950) was to some extent a reaction to the *Methodenstreit*, but also to the dangers of fascism and communism. Eucken wanted to overcome the "great antinomies" expressed in the dispute via a "third way." The centrally administered economy of the Soviet Union and the tyranny of National Socialist Germany spurred him to develop a conception of order positioned between capitalism and socialism. The goal was a durable and well-functioning economic order that combined individual freedom with social justice and sought to reconcile conflicting interests. Competition and social welfare policies were the supporting pillars of this order— a "mixed system." Ideas of ordoliberalism were influential in Germany in the aftermath of World War II and gave rise to the concept of "social market economy" elaborated by the economist Alfred Müller-Armack (1901–1978). The concept was taken up by Ludwig Erhard (1897–1977), minister for economic affairs in the Federal Republic of Germany from 1949 to 1963, who earned himself the title "father of the German economic miracle" (postwar Germany's rise to economic prosperity). Echoes of ordoliberal ideas are also discernible in the economic and political architecture of the European Union.

The American Economic Association (AEA) was cofounded in 1885 by Richard T. Ely (1854–1943), educated in the German historical school and holding a German PhD. Ely was keen to shape the AEA in the image of the German Verein für Socialpolitik, founded by the historicists in 1873, but had to succumb to colleagues who opted for a more open and theory-based approach to economics. Historicism appears to have had a negligible long-term impact on the American economics profession, although more recent developments and especially the way in which statistics and econometrics are frequently used may be interpreted as a revival of historicism in a new garb, equipped with powerful tools of quantitative analysis. In such works, economic theory no longer informs econometrics by suggesting analytically derived relationships between economic magnitudes that should be empirically tested. Rather, it is econometrics that informs economic analysis by drawing attention to existing dependencies between some such magnitudes.

MARIE-ESPRIT-LÉON WALRAS Léon Walras, an economist who taught in Lausanne, Switzerland, had a major long-term impact on the field with his *Éléments d'économie politique pure*, published in two parts in 1874 and 1877. Walras was the point of departure for the theory of general economic equilibrium. He understood the "pure science of economics" as the analysis of ideal types that are conceptualized by abstracting from real types and whose interactions are analyzed with mathematical methods. Only when a science defined this way was "completed," maintained Walras, should the path back to reality be pursued, so that practical problems in "applied economics" can be solved on a theoretical foundation. The contrast to the historical school could not be greater.

According to Walras, the first major problem of a "mathematical theory of social wealth" involves pure exchange (with which Jevons, and before him Turgot, had already dealt). Two persons are endowed with initial sets of two goods. Can both increase their welfare by exchanging portions of their stock of goods with each other? And at what relative price? The individual maximizes his utility whenever the marginal utility—Walras uses the word *rareté*—divided by the price of the good is the same in relation to all goods. (We recognize this as Gossen's second law.) For every agent, moreover, and setting aside credit, the value of his sales must correspond to the value of his purchases. This must also hold for the aggregate, the overall economy: the sum of sales must equal the sum of purchases. To put it another way: if $n - 1$ markets are in equilibrium, meaning that if the sum of sales is equal to that of purchases on these markets, then the nth market must also be in equilibrium. Thus, only $n - 1$ of the equations expressing equilibrium are independent of one another. This is referred to as "Walras's law."

The second major problem, insisted Walras, concerns price formation for consumer goods. These are subject to the "law of the cost of production or of the cost price." Walras assumed that all goods are produced with fixed input quantities of "productive services" per unit generated: labor, land, and capital services. Four sets of equations comprise the system of general equilibrium: (1) equations that describe the supplies of different productive services as dependent on the relative prices of all goods and services, (2) equations that describe consumer demand as dependent on relative prices, (3) equations that express the equality of amounts of productive services supplied and demanded, and finally (4) equations that express the equality of prices and production costs for consumer goods. Since the number of equations is equal to the number of unknowns, Walras concluded that he had found a "theoretical solution" to "the same problem which is solved in practice by the market by the mechanism of free competition." If several methods for producing the different goods are available, competition will see to it that the cost-minimizing one will be selected.

The third major problem with the mathematical theory of social wealth, as Walras saw it, concerns the price formation of capital goods. This refers to durable capital goods that wear out as they are used and periodically need to be replaced and that yield their owners a "net income" (gross profits minus depreciation) for their productive services. In equilibrium, according to Walras, net income relative to the price of a brand-new unit of a capital good is uniform across all capital goods. There is thus a close connection between the price of the durable capital good and that of its productive service. A uniform rate of net income in conditions of free competition echoes, of course, the uniform rate of profits in classical economics.

Moreover, the price of a brand-new capital good obeys the "law of production costs." This leads to a fifth set of equations whereby the prices of capital goods are equal to their production costs. The number of additional equations is now, however, smaller by one than the number of additional unknowns (prices of capital goods and net income rate or profit rate). Walras tried to close the system by means of an additional equation that expresses an equilibrium between gross savings and gross investments and contains no new unknowns. By means of this additional equation, he surmised, it should now be possible to determine, along with all the other unknowns, not only the competitive rate of profits but also the overall rate of capital accumulation (capitalization) and thus how much the economy grows from one year to the next.

TÂTONNEMENT It was clear to Walras that equilibrium is not always established immediately. Why, then, is there a tendency to equilibrium in markets? Why are markets supposed to be "stable"? This is the subject of the concept he called *tâtonnement*, a "groping" or trial-and-error movement toward equilibrium. The basic idea can be illustrated by using the figure of an auctioneer. For all tradable goods, an auctioneer shouts out a set of arbitrary price quotes (*crié au hasard*). Firms and households list the amounts they intend to buy and sell at these prices. The auctioneer collects the information and adds up the relevant amounts for each market. If he finds out that the markets are not all simultaneously in equilibrium, he shouts out new prices, which he sets in the following way: with regard to those things in which the collective supply exceeds the demand (excess supply), he lowers the price, and conversely (for excess demand), he increases the price. Once again, the agents announce how much they want to buy and sell, and the process continues.

Walras was confident that the process would always converge toward general equilibrium, meaning that it is globally stable. He considered the "law of supply and demand" to be comparable to the law of universal gravitation in astronomy. Walras assumed that trading could only happen when the equilibrium quote of prices had been found—there are no transactions at what future economists would call "false prices."

THE RECEPTION OF WALRAS'S WORK Schumpeter called Walras's theory the Magna Carta of economics. Schumpeter's former teacher and advocate of the "causal-genetic method" Eugen von Böhm-Bawerk, by contrast, saw the method of simultaneous equations as "a mortal sin against all scientific logic."

As impressive as the Walrasian construct is, it has obvious weaknesses. Does the system even have a solution? If so, is it economically meaningful? An equal number of unknowns and equations does not guarantee a solution: if the equations contradict one another, then there is no solution. And should there be one, it could include negative prices, which make no economic sense. There is also no reason to assume that, for a given initial endowment of the economy with productive resources, all resources will be fully employed. Some can be in excess supply and lie fallow. The relevant conditions of equilibrium would then have to be described as weak *in*equalities rather than as equations. But what if the amount of a resource that is available is greater than the amount in demand? Then, according to Walrasian logic, its price must fall to zero. But can wages, for example, fall to zero? And if yes, what then?

In brief: Walras's assumption of a given initial endowment is at best compatible with a short-period equilibrium, characterized by differential rates of profit, but not, as he believed, with a long-period one. His treatment of the problem of capital formation is also not tenable. The equality between the sum total of savings and the sum total of investments, which Walras was convinced allowed him to determine the rate of profits and the rate of capital accumulation, does not in fact settle the problem. The reason is simple: to obtain a solution it is not enough to have the macroeconomic equality under discussion; one must know also the composition of investment demand—the amounts of specific capital goods making up investments. But this is left in the open. Without knowing how much of each of these capital goods will be produced, overall output quantities of the various goods cannot be ascertained, and neither can prices of goods and productive services.

Walras's theory was the point of departure for several developments in the field, trying to make good the lacunae Walras left behind. Vilfredo Pareto (1848–1923), in his *Manuale di economia politica* (1906), and Gustav Cassel (1866–1945), in his *Theory of Social Economy* (1918), shared Walras's interest in determining a long-period equilibrium characterized by a uniform rate of profits. This necessitated giving up the assumption of a capital endowment of the economy in terms of arbitrarily given amounts of heterogeneous capital goods (spades, ploughs, tractors, computers, etc.). Only in the case in which there was just a single type of capital good like Ricardo's wheat could the long-period method be retained—hardly a realistic and interesting case. Otherwise the capital endowment had to be given as a sum of value with its physical composition determined as a part of the solution of the system (as in the case of Wicksell, mentioned earlier).

This was not very satisfactory, and some authors soon began to search for ways to avoid the impasse by abandoning the concept of long-period equilibrium and replacing it with that of short-period equilibria. There are two kinds of such equilibrium concepts—that of temporary equilibrium of Erik Lindahl (1891–1960) and John Hicks (1904–1989), on the one hand, and that of intertemporal equilibrium of Lindahl and Hayek, on the other. The latter had its pinnacle in the works of Kenneth Arrow (b. 1921) and Gérard Debreu (1921–2004). We deal briefly with their contributions in chapter 11.

5

MARSHALL AND THE THEORY
OF PARTIAL EQUILIBRIUM

A lfred Marshall's *Principles of Economics* (1890) is one of the most influential books on economics ever written. The method of partial equilibria it develops is omnipresent even today and shapes the idea of economics as the science of supply and demand. At the same time, Marshall cannot be reduced to this one idea; on the contrary. He wrote that "the Mecca of the economist lies in economic biology rather than in economic dynamics," with "dynamics" in this case denoting an approach more mechanistic (in the sense of Newton's astronomy) than evolutionary. If the "evolutionist" aspect of Marshall's work does not come up for discussion in greater detail here, this is because today's mainstream economics sees the mechanical—not the biological—as of paramount importance.

Marshall's success in regard to partial equilibrium analysis has many causes, including the easy teachability of the supply-and-demand theory. Marshall maintained that everything that can be explained with the aid of mathematics should also be expressible in words (with the help of diagrams) or else it is no good; this attitude goes a long way toward lowering the cost of entry into his work. Students and practitioners, he insisted, should be able to read it. In addition, Marshall (in contrast especially to Jevons) did not present this theory as a drastic or even revolutionary innovation but rather as a continuation of the classical tradition, although scrutiny shows that it involved a fundamental break with the classical approach. But as plausible and straightforward as demand-and-supply curves may appear at first glance, they turn out to be extremely tricky on closer inspection.

PARTIAL ANALYSIS According to Marshall, economics, given the complexity of its area of study, is closed off to controlled experiments (a limitation that advocates of experimental economics have recently been trying to overcome; see chap. 12). Marshall also saw the function of analysis as "not to forge a few long chains of reasoning, but to forge rightly many short chains." This methodological position, formulated against the "long chain" of general equilibrium theory, led Marshall to study individual markets on the assumption that the prices of all other goods and productive services are given and constant. This is the "method of partial equilibria." Marshall focused attention on the case of perfect competition—the workhorse of much of marginalist economics. He postulated strict conditions under which partial equilibrium methods may be applied: (1) demand-and-supply curves need to be independent of each other, (2) only small changes in price or quantity are allowed for, and (3) adjustments triggered by some change must be restricted to the market under observation and must not influence noticeably the situation in other markets. Alas, these conditions have been widely disregarded, implying a huge overestimation of the explanatory power of the partial equilibrium method and an unwarranted reliance on policy recommendations derived from it.

PERIOD ANALYSIS Marshall addressed the problem of the determination of prices and quantities produced by way of a "period analysis." In an extremely short-run view (a day at the fish market comes to mind), the supply is fixed and demand determines the market price. In a short-run view (say, a week at the fish market), the supply can be varied within certain limits by changing the capacity utilization of machines and the intensity of work (or the time a boat and its crew spend fishing); in this case, then, both demand and supply have an impact on the short-run normal price. In a long-run view, the production apparatus and employment can be varied (in the case of a fishery: the number of boats and crews can be changed), and the number of firms in the market can also change (that is, new firms could enter into or exit from the fishing industry). In determining the long-run normal price, therefore, supply is still more influential relative to demand. In a very-long-run or secular view, technological and organizational changes will have to be taken into account, that is, the new knowledge incorporated into new capital goods and labor determines the price via the simultaneous change of supply and demand (in the case of a fishery, think of the introduction of sonar fish-finding devices).

Marshall's concept of the long-run normal price bears a strong resemblance to the classical concept of the production price, and like the classicists he postulated a uniform rate of return on capital in competitive conditions. He granted that the classical economists had done a good job developing the production side, yet he faulted them for their alleged neglect of the demand side. In order to determine price, as he put it in a famous metaphor, "the two blades of a scissors"— demand and supply—are usually required.

In order to better understand Marshall's idea, let us look at a single firm in the short run. Under conditions of perfect competition, it has no market power whatsoever and must accept the price it finds in the market. The firm confronts a marginal cost function relating cost per unit of output and output. Cost typically increases with output: the production of each additional unit tends to be more expensive than the unit produced just before. The reason for this is that in the short run the firm is constrained by given fixed factors of production: a given plant and equipment, a given workforce, and the like. Only some factors vary, such as the amount of raw materials that are being processed and the amount of energy that is being used. With an increasing level of output the relative scarcity of the fixed factors will translate into rising costs per unit of output—that is, rising marginal costs. (The share of nonvendible output or waste may increase as workers get tired and so on.) The firm is now assumed to maximize its profits at that production volume at which its marginal costs are equal to the price. If the price were higher, ceteris paribus, the firm would supply a greater quantity. This leads to the concept of a "supply function" for the firm. It is equal to the marginal cost function of the firm (above the minimum of average variable costs). Since the number of firms is assumed to be constant in the short run, Marshall aggregates the firm-specific supply functions and so arrives at the supply curve for the entire industry producing the good in question.

As regards the construction of the corresponding demand curve, the argument is the following. Individuals are seen to have given needs and wants, which they can satisfy with different combinations of goods. In other words, there is the possibility of substituting one good for another one and yet obtaining the same satisfaction or utility. For example, rice can be substituted for potatoes (and vice versa). For given prices of all goods except one, an increase (or decrease) in the price of this good will typically (albeit not necessarily) prompt the individual to consume less (or more) of it. This leads to the concept of the demand function of the consumer, which relates the quantity demanded and alternative levels of the price of the good under consideration, taking the prices of all other goods (and also the income of the consumer) as constant. Aggregating the demand functions of all consumers with respect to the good gives the collective demand function. It is typically (but not necessarily) assumed to show that the lower the price of the good, the higher the quantity demanded.

Marshall then confronts the collective supply curve with the collective demand curve and locates at the intersection of the two curves the equilibrium price and the equilibrium quantity. In figure 5.1 the quantity is plotted

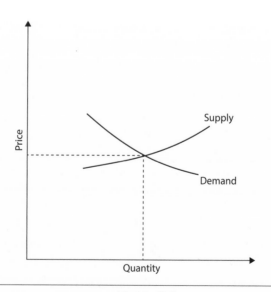

FIGURE 5.1 The Marshallian cross

along the x-axis and the price along the y-axis, as is now conventional. Here I have drawn the supply and the demand curves for small changes in price and quantity only, following Marshall's condition 2. In textbooks one frequently encounters curves drawn for huge intervals of prices (and quantities), say, from $1 to $1,000. But imagine the price of rice in India jumps to fifty times its present value: in this case one better forget equilibrium analysis and turn to a theory of political unrest and revolution.

The long-run analysis needs to take into account that some of the incumbent firms may leave the market and new ones may enter it and the overall number of firms and thus the productive capacity of the industry may change. If the price is greater than the minimum of average costs, then the firms that are in the market get extra profits. This attracts additional firms. In the reverse case, firms in the market take losses and depart. The only price that can be an equilibrium price for the firm is obviously equal to the long-term minimum of average costs.

What does the long-run equilibrium of an industry look like? This depends on how production costs develop along with changes in the production volume of an industry. In the long run, ideally, all productive factors are variable—there are no fixed factors. For example, while in the short run the firm may be constrained by the size of its plant and equipment and the number of skilled workers, in the long run it can increase (or decrease) the former by net investment (or disinvestment) and the latter by hiring more (or fewer) workers. Hence in the long run firms can adjust their productive capacity to match the quantities they wish to bring to the market. The question, then, is whether the firm operates under constant, decreasing, or increasing "returns to scale." By this, economists mean whether an increase in output is brought about by a proportional, more than proportional, or less then proportional increase in the various inputs. With given input prices this translates into unit costs that are constant, increasing, or decreasing.

Only when costs per unit are constant, regardless of the production volume, is the long-run supply curve a straight line parallel to the quantity axis. Demand then determines only the volume produced by the industry, but not the price, which is cost determined. In the case of increasing marginal and average costs, the assumption that all factors are variable does not apply. The industry may, for example, use a particular type of land that is in short supply, and when the industry's output grows, the growing relative scarcity of the land will be reflected in higher rents paid to the owners of the land (which contradicts the assumption of constant prices of all other goods and inputs). In the case of falling marginal and average costs at rising production volume, Marshall distinguishes between economies of scale that are internal to the firm and economies that are external to the firm. In the former case the economies apply to single firms only, not to the industry as a whole, while in the latter case they apply simultaneously to all firms within the industry. That is, the industry as a whole benefits from larger output levels. In the case in which the economies are internal to the firm, a monopoly forms. This is so because a firm that happens to produce a larger output has a cost advantage over its competitors and is able to drive them out of the market. The larger the output of the firm the lower are its unit costs and the greater is its capability to undercut the prices of its competitors.

This case eludes the Marshallian analysis of equilibrium in a competitive economy. Only the case of economies that are internal to the industry but external to the single firm would be captured by his theory, but Marshall has difficulty identifying convincing empirical examples for this. Since he attaches great importance to this case, he attempts to keep it within the purview of his theory by introducing positive "external effects." These kinds of effects accompany the growth of an industry and lower the average costs of all firms in that industry, even though each individual firm, taken on its own, exhibits rising costs; external effects evade control by the individual firm. Marshall illustrates his concept of increasing returns that are internal to an industry in terms of the improved level of information that accompanies the expansion of an industry in a restricted geographic space ("industrial districts"). Think of the agglomeration of firms producing similar products such as cars or machine tools in a particular region. In modern times, the IT and high-technology industry in Silicon Valley comes to one's mind.

In the case of costs dependent on quantity ("variable" costs), the long-term supply curve of an industry can, in principle, exhibit a rising or a falling slope, depending on whether decreasing or increasing returns prevail.

SRAFFA'S CRITIQUE Piero Sraffa subjected partial analysis to a thoroughgoing critique in two essays published in 1925 and 1926. His main objections are: it cannot be ruled out that a change in the production volume of an industry with variable costs simultaneously changes the costs of firms in other industries. This contradicts Marshall's condition 3. This is the case, for example, when both industries use the same kind of land to produce different goods, for example, apples and pears. An increase in the production of apples drives up the rent of land. But this shifts the cost function of both apples and pears upward. In addition, if the increased production of apples leads to a change in the cost situation of firms that make inputs for producing apples (for example, fertilizers or harvesting machines), this has repercussions for the cost function in apple production.

Both cases are incompatible with the independence of supply functions in different industries from one another, and they cast doubt on the applicability of partial analysis. If a change in the production volume of an industry with variable costs does not occasion changes in the costs of firms in other industries, then the variable costs are internal to the industry. This is, for example, the case when each and every particular type of land is used in the production of just a single type of commodity. (For example, only land of quality A is used in apple production, whereas only land of quality B is used in pear production.) But since this case is not very important empirically, Sraffa concluded that while demand does not affect price in the case of constant returns and thus constant unit costs, given all input prices, the case of variable costs is either incompatible with the assumption of competition (if increasing returns are internal to the firm), or it falls out of the scope of partial analysis and requires a general analysis, or it is difficult to provide compelling empirical evidence in support of it. The explanatory value of the analysis is, accordingly, extremely small.

Because of the interdependencies between industries, it is simply not possible in general to change the price of just one input or output at a time and analyze the effect of such a change in a single market as if in a vacuum. There are always repercussions within the economic system that may not only quantitatively but also qualitatively affect the result. Partial equilibrium analysis thus ought to be employed with great caution, and its results should be adopted only after careful examination within a more general framework of the analysis. Sraffa's criticism was widely discussed at the time. Joseph A. Schumpeter spoke of Sraffa's "brilliantly original performance." Oskar Morgenstern (1902–1977), originally an advocate of the Austrian variant of marginalism, concluded from Sraffa's criticism (1) that "the method of partial equilibrium has been blown up" and (2) the alleged symmetry of demand and supply is doubtful. If with respect to small changes in output it is best to start from constant returns in long-run analysis, as Sraffa had argued, the importance of the demand side and Marshall's approach as such are called into question.

There are a few possible reactions to Sraffa's critique. First, one abandons the method of partial equilibrium but sticks to the demand-and-supply approach in conditions of perfect competition. In this case a general equilibrium framework has to be adopted, in which interdependencies among the various agents and industries of the economy are taken into consideration. I deal with such contributions in chapters 6 and 11. Second, one abandons both the partial equilibrium method and the demand-and-supply approach and returns to the surplus approach of the classical economists. This also involves a general analytical framework that takes into account independencies among industries. I deal with contributions to the respective literature in chapter 12. Third, one gives up on the assumption of perfect competition but preserves the partial equilibrium framework. This leads to theories of imperfect or monopolistic competition, in which attention shifts to various market forms. To these theories I turn briefly in chapter 7. But before doing so I summarize in great brevity some important trends and debates in economics toward the end of the nineteenth and in the first half of the twentieth century.

6

UTILITARIANISM, WELFARE THEORY, AND SYSTEMS DEBATE

Around the turn of the nineteenth century, marginalist theory consolidated and branched out, especially in the different forms of utilitarianism that underlie it as well as in the development of welfare theory. The "greatest happiness of the greatest number" (Francis Hutcheson, Jeremy Bentham) or the "maximum satisfaction" (Marshall) of the needs of a society's members had long preoccupied economists. It was now taken up again and analyzed within the confines of the new theory, based on marginal utility and marginal productivity. At around the same time the socialist movement gained momentum and challenged capitalism—with the foundation of the Soviet Union providing a widely visible alternative to it. As a consequence a debate arose about which economic system was superior: capitalism or socialism. We deal first with the development of marginalist theory and then turn to the debate regarding the two systems.

FRANCIS YSIDRO EDGEWORTH Utilitarianism had been a focus of some economists since Jeremy Bentham (1748–1832) introduced the concept. The goal of Edgeworth (1845–1926) was to give utilitarianism an "exact" form; see especially his two books *New and Old Methods of Ethics* (1877) and *Mathematical Psychics: An Essay on the Application of Mathematics to the Moral Sciences* (1881). While Edgeworth conceded that, strictly speaking, utility cannot be measured and cannot be compared interpersonally, he felt that for practical purposes it is admissible to assume that it can. He transposed the finding of the German psychologist Gustav Fechner (1801–1887) that perception of a sensual stimulation increases less than proportionally as its intensity grows to the connection between marginal utility and the income an individual receives. The result was the law of the diminishing marginal utility of income: from a certain point onward the higher one's income, the smaller the increase in utility from each additional unit of currency.

The corresponding concept of cardinal utility, which Edgeworth advocated, did not mean only that the consumer is able to decide whether one bundle of goods has greater utility than another one, but also how much greater this utility is. Edgeworth's "exact utilitarianism" implied that in the case of similar perceptions of utility among individuals, a more equitable distribution of income increases the welfare of society as a whole: the marginal utility of income is low for the rich, high for the poor, and redistribution in favor of the latter may increase total utility.

Unlike Gossen and Jevons, Edgeworth did not assume a so-called additive utility function; instead, he allowed that the amount of a good consumed has an impact on the marginal utility derived from the consumption of other goods. Rau and the Austrian economists Rudolf Auspitz (1837–1906) and Richard Lieben (1842–1919) subsequently distinguished between "complementary" and "substitute" goods. Complementary goods can only be used together, as for example, a car and fuel or a pipe and tobacco. Substitutive goods are goods that can replace each other, as for example, rice and potatoes or a fountain pen and a ballpoint pen. An increase in the price (ceteris paribus) of a complementary good will result in a decrease in demand also for the other good, and a decrease will correspondingly result in an increase in demand for both goods. For a substitute good, it is the opposite; an increase in price will result in an increase in demand for the other good, and a decrease in price will result in a decrease in demand for the other good. In more technical terms: if the consumption of a small additional amount of one of two goods increases the marginal utility of the other good, then we are dealing with complementary goods; if it decreases marginal utility, they are substitutive goods. Underlying this formulation is the concept of "cross price elasticity," which relates the relative change in the demand for one good to the relative change in the price of another good. It answers the question: By what percent does the demand for good X change when the price of good Y increases ceteris paribus by 1 percent? As we have said, if the demand for X falls then we have complementary goods, and if it rises we have substitute goods. The magnitude of the percentage change in demand provides information about the level of complementarity or substitutability between the two goods under consideration.

Edgeworth was the first to introduce the concept of the "indifference curve," which gives all those combinations of quantities of two goods that are each of equally great utility for the individual. Drawing a diagram with the quantity of good X consumed along the x-axis and the quantity of good Y along the y-axis, strictly complementary goods are reflected in indifference curves that look like an "L" with the optimal combination of the two goods given by the corner of the L (fig. 6.1A). Starting from there and adding a little to the quantity of any one of the two goods while leaving the amount of the other one constant does not increase (or decrease) utility. To the left and to the right of the corner of the L the indifference curve therefore is parallel to each of the two axes. In the case of substitute goods the indifference curve is downward sloping. In the extreme it is a straight line, which means that the two goods are perfect substitutes (fig. 6.1B). If the indifference curve has neither the shape of an L nor that of a straight line, the two goods can be substituted more or less easily for one another (fig. 6.1C). The ease (or difficulty) with which they can be substituted generally depends, of course, on the point on the indifference curve at which the substitution should take place. The more one good (for example, Y) has already replaced the other one (X), given the overall utility level, the more difficult it gets to further replace X by Y, that is, an ever-larger additional amount of Y must be made available to compensate a given reduction of the consumed quantity of X. In figure 6.1C compare the slopes of the indifference curve in points A and B to see this. In other words, it becomes always dearer in terms of good Y to replace good X, leaving the utility level of the consumer unaffected. This is known as the falling marginal rate of substitution of good Y for good X.

VILFREDO PARETO Pareto rejected the concept of cardinal utility and replaced it with one that is ordinal: although one can say whether a bundle

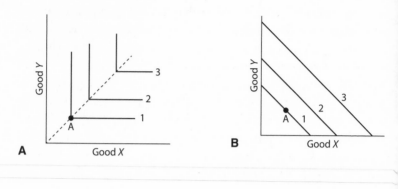

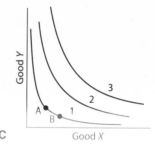

FIGURE 6.1 Indifference curves: complements and substitutes

of goods is preferred or subordinated to another, one cannot say by how much. Utility, also, cannot be compared between and aggregated across individuals. Seen from this point of view, neither the concept of a falling marginal utility of income nor the concept of the collective utility of a society as a whole makes sense. In order to distinguish his views from traditional utilitarian ideas, Pareto replaced the concept of "utility" with that of "ophelimity" (*ophélimité*).

Does the "ordinal revolution" of utility theory, as it was dubbed, render the marginalist theory of demand invalid? By no means, according to Pareto. One can get by without the concept of cardinal utility, in Pareto's view, and instead consider a bundle of indifference curves for an individual. From these it is possible to derive the individual's preferences as well as his or her demand for goods at a given income and given prices.

In discussing the case of pure exchange, Pareto invented a graphical device that is wrongly attributed to Edgeworth: the so-called Edgeworth box. Take two individuals, each initially endowed with given amounts of two goods. Pareto's question was: Is it possible for the two to exchange parts of their endowments in a way that is mutually beneficial, in the sense that it allows each individual to increase his or her utility level above the level attainable by consuming the initial endowment? In other words: Are there (utility) gains from pure exchange or trade? Pareto showed that, in general, there are numerous exchange equilibria and corresponding price ratios of the two goods, ranging from a situation in which the entire advantage of exchange rests with one individual to the opposite case. In between there is an array of equilibria in which both have an advantage; all such equilibria lie along the "contract curve." This curve marks the points at which one individual can improve his or her situation only at the cost of the other individual. This is the so-called Pareto optimality, when resources are allocated in such a way that it is impossible to better the situation of one individual without worsening that of another.

How does the consumer react when the price of a good changes, everything else being equal? We have already touched upon this question when dealing with complementary and substitute goods. Here we deepen the analysis somewhat, allowing the reader another look into the laboratory of the economists and how they elaborated the concepts under consideration.

Their thought experiments started from the ceteris paribus assumption. On its basis they constructed what are known as "demand functions." A demand function relates the demand for a good to the good's price. In the thought experiment, the price varies while the prices of all other goods and wages, profits, rents, and so on are given and assumed to be constant. A hypothetical consumer with preferences typically represented by a utility function is then "asked" how his or her demand for the good changes given the change in price. The economist plots these "answers" in a diagram.

INCOME AND SUBSTITUTION EFFECT In the case of so-called normal goods, demand rises when the price falls, and vice versa. But this need not be the case for every good and with respect to every price change.

As the Russian economist Eugen Slutsky (1880–1948) and later John Hicks showed, the impact of a ceteris paribus change in the price of a good can be decomposed into two partial effects. Let us exemplify the argument for the case in which the price of the good is increased. This makes the good more expensive relative to all other goods, which leads, for a given level of utility, to a reduced demand for this good and an increased demand for one or several other goods. This is the "substitution effect." On the other hand, the price increase for the good means a smaller real income—the consumer can afford less than before. Depending on the importance of the good under discussion for the consumer, the demand for it will fall or rise. This is the "income effect."

The sum of both effects describes how demand from an individual reacts to an increase in price. The substitution effect, as it is defined here, is invariably negative, whereas the income effect is either negative or positive. In the case of normal goods it is negative—with a decrease in income the demand for the good decreases (and with an increase in income it increases)—whereas in the case of so-called inferior goods the income effect is positive: the demand for such goods increases with a decrease in income. Inferior goods are goods that, with growing incomes, are replaced by higher-estimated goods, for example, potatoes are replaced by meat, and vice versa with decreasing incomes. An extreme case is the "Giffen good," named after the Scottish statistician Robert Giffen (1837–1910), the demand for which increases at an increase in its price. Explained in terms of the decomposition of the overall effect we may now say that a Giffen good is an inferior good for which the income effect, which is positive, dominates the substitution effect, which is negative.

THE FUNDAMENTAL THEOREMS OF WELFARE ECONOMICS

Pareto's theory of the demand for goods is a building block of his theory of general equilibrium and his welfare theory. General equilibrium theory typically starts from three sets of data, or givens, or independent variables (see chap. 4): (1) given preferences of agents; (2) given technical alternatives to produce the various commodities; and (3) given initial endowments of the economy of productive factors and given property rights of agents. Pareto showed that under certain restrictive assumptions regarding, especially, production technology and preferences, there exists a market equilibrium that is Pareto optimal. Paul A. Samuelson called this outcome the "first fundamental theorem of welfare economics." Pareto also showed that by redistributing initial endowments among agents, any (feasible) equilibrium, and along with it any (feasible) Pareto optimum, can be brought about. Samuelson referred to this as the "second fundamental theorem of welfare economics."

These two theorems, developed within the framework of ordinal utility theory, replace the discussion of a redistribution of income (and wealth) based on a falling marginal utility of income and derived within a cardinal framework, as we encountered it in the work of Edgeworth (and will do so again in that of Arthur Cecil Pigou, discussed in a later section). Compared with cardinal utility theory, ordinal utility theory—with its rejection of interpersonal comparisons—dramatically privileges the individual relative to society. In this perspective the individual, one might say, is in principle attributed a right to veto public decisions that affect his or her (subjective) well-being. In such a situation it seems almost impossible to say whether situation A is better for society than situation B. As a consequence, economic policy seems unable to improve social situations. Since every policy alternative has some gainers and some losers, how could one ever judge the gains of the former against the losses of the latter, if interpersonal utility comparisons are prohibited?

THE KALDOR-HICKS COMPENSATION CRITERION A way out of this cul-de-sac was suggested by Nicholas Kaldor and John Hicks in essays published in 1939. Kaldor took the case of the repeal of the English Corn Laws in 1846 to exemplify his suggested solution. He argued that the repeal harmed the landed gentry because of a fall in rents due to the importation of cheap corn from abroad. It benefited the consumers because of a fall in the price of corn and as a consequence also in that of bread. (Ricardo had already opposed the Corn Laws. He had argued that their repeal would benefit first and foremost capitalists because of a rise in the general rate of profits and, as a consequence, society at large because of a rise in the rate of capital accumulation and growth.) If those who gain from the repeal could in principle (that is, in theory) compensate those who lose, and still remain better off, then the repeal is desirable for society. There is no need for the compensation actually to take place. The Kaldor-Hicks compensation criterion focuses attention on the abstract possibility of compensation payments. A Pareto improvement results from a policy in which no one is worse off and some people are better off. Against the background of this concept, the Kaldor-Hicks criterion informs us about whether a policy option involves a potential Pareto improvement.

The Kaldor-Hicks criterion gave rise to a debate to which, among others, the Hungarian-born American economist Tibor Scitovsky (1910–2002) and Paul Samuelson contributed and in which different compensation criteria were proposed. It turned out that without constant relative prices of goods and very similar consumers with very special preferences the compensation criteria all fared badly. (We briefly come back to welfare theory in chap. 11.)

PERSONAL INCOME DISTRIBUTION AND THE LORENZ CURVE

Pareto also drew the attention to an important empirical finding regarding the personal distribution of income, that is, the distribution of income among individuals or families, irrespective of the source(s) of their income (wages, profits, rents, interest, etc.): this is the "Pareto principle," also known as the 80–20 rule. According to this principle, 20 percent of the population receives 80 percent of income, and 20 percent of these 20 percent in turn have 80 percent of this 80 percent, and so on. Incomes are accordingly very unequally distributed. Over time the inequality of income distribution may decrease or even increase both in single countries and worldwide. While transnational inequality on a global scale has been reduced in recent times, due to the rapid economic development of populous countries like China or India, inequality inside many countries has risen sharply.

Analogous observations can be made about wealth, consumption, energy use, and so on. If, in a diagram with one axis showing shares of population (from zero to one) and the other showing shares of national income (from zero to one), one registers the corresponding empirical values (x percent of the population receives y percent of income), one obtains the "Lorenz curve," named after the American statistician Max Otto Lorenz (1876–1959) (fig. 6.2). If income were equally distributed, there would be a straight line linking the points [0, 0] and [1, 1]. The stronger the bend of the curve, the greater the inequality of the distribution.

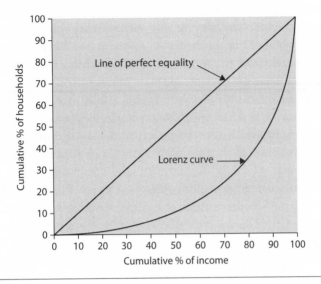

FIGURE 6.2 The Lorenz curve

The "Gini coefficient" (between 0 und 1), named after the Italian stat-istician Corrado Gini (1884–1965), is a measure of the deviation of the Lorenz curve from the straight line that indicates an equal distribution of income. Countries like the United States and China exhibit relatively high (and rising) Gini coefficients, greater than 0.6, while the coefficients for European, and especially Scandinavian, countries are significantly lower. Major research on income and wealth distribution is due to the work of the British economist Anthony B. Atkinson (b. 1944) and the French econo-mist Thomas Piketty (b. 1971). In his book *Capital in the 21st Century*, pub-lished in English in 2014, Piketty argues that the redistribution of income and wealth in favor of the rich and the super-rich even more so tends to undermine the foundations upon which Western societies are erected—the belief that what matters for an individual's economic and social success is hard work and high productivity. The ideal is a meritocratic society, in which the American dream is possible—everyone can in principle "make it," can rise from the proverbial dishwasher to a billionaire. This presup-poses that the opportunities of social advancement are intact and that there is permeability among different social strata. While there are certain extreme examples of this, they are relatively few. Pareto's empirical research already established that the circulation of elites is low. Piketty's book confirms this and points to the danger of gradually sliding from a relatively meritocratic society into a more and more patrimonial one, in which what matters is largely whether a person is born or marries into a wealthy family and not so much how hardworking or productive the person is. Piketty and Atkinson therefore advocate taxing inheritances and wealth more generally to avoid the return of quasi-feudal times and secure similar opportunities for the young.

I will conclude by saying that Pareto was aware of the limited range covered by the fictional character of *homo economicus* and of the theory of equilibrium based on that artificial construct. He was convinced that economics alone could not satisfactorily explain social phenomena. Late in life he turned to sociology and with his *Trattato di sociologia generale* (1916), composed a classic work in the discipline.

ARTHUR CECIL PIGOU Pigou (1877–1959) was a representative of the Marshallian theory of partial equilibrium, and his simplifications of the argument and novel ideas granted him lasting success. Like Marshall, he was interested above all in the practical application of theory to the improvement of human living conditions; see in particular his book *The Economics of Welfare* (1920). He did not share Pareto's critique of the concept of cardinal utility and of the "law of the diminishing marginal utility of income." And so, in principle, he advocated a redistribution of income favoring the recipients of smaller incomes, with the proviso that this must not violate Marshall's principle of "welfare maximization": this means *yes* to redistribution, so long as it does not diminish overall welfare. His reversion to a pre-Pareto position earned Pigou harsh criticism from his London colleague Lionel Robbins, who in his *Essay on the Nature and Significance of Economic Science* (1932) developed an alternative program to Pigou's reflections on welfare theory. But the idea that all human beings should be assigned something close to equal weight in economic considerations proved ineradicable, and today it is a regular feature of studies on distributive questions, the problem of poverty, and the problem of intergenerational justice.

Pigou had a major impact on the way public finance is taught today with his book *A Study in Public Finance* (1928). He is perhaps most famous for his treatment of the problem of "negative" and "positive" externalities. An example of the former is a producer who channels pollutants into a river and damages the fishing community there; an example of the latter would be a beekeeper whose bees pollinate the blossoms of a neighboring floriculturist. In both cases, there is a cost or benefit that affects unrelated third parties. When the costs arising from environmental pollution or the benefits arising from bees' pollination are not imputed to the person causing them—economists speak of the "internalization" of costs or benefits—private marginal costs and benefits do not equal social ones and we arrive at a misallocation of resources and undesirable distribution effects. In order to bring about an equality of private and social marginal costs and benefits, Pigou proposed in the first case a tax on production (Pigouvian tax) whose value is equal to the costs otherwise arising for the general public, and in the second case a subsidy (Pigouvian subsidy) that is equal to the benefit accruing to the general public. Pigou also applied Gossen's second law to public finance: the social utility of the last unit of a resource deployed should be equally large, in every direction, whether private or public.

Pigou revived the idea of an "optimal system of taxation," whose roots can be traced far back in the history of economic thought. At his suggestion, his young Cambridge colleague Frank Plumpton Ramsey (1903–1930)—a brilliant philosopher and mathematician—elaborated a mathematical model of optimal taxation that was the point of departure for an extensive literature on the subject.

In his book *The Theory of Unemployment* (1933), Pigou argued that under conditions of perfect competition, all markets (including the labor market) tend toward being cleared, that is, to an equilibrium between demand and supply. One reason he advanced is that in a depression, the drop in price level causes the real value of (outside) money to increase, which stimulates consumption (the so-called Pigou effect). ("Outside money" is money that is not a liability for some economic subject within the economy; money issued by central banks is typically considered outside money.) In his *General Theory* (1936), Keynes rejected Pigou's view in light of the world economic crisis and mass unemployment—but by doing so he presented Pigou's analysis in a way that served his critical purpose. Pigou was certainly no supporter of a deflationary policy attempting to achieve a higher level of employment via falling prices and wages. It deserves also to be mentioned that we find in Pigou formulations that foreshadow certain macroeconomic ideas, although they were not expressed in a clear-cut manner, one example being the concept of the "multiplier" put forward by Richard Kahn (1905–1989) and then adopted by Keynes (see chap. 10).

CAPITALISM OR SOCIALISM? This question was posed at the beginning of the twentieth century in what has been called the "great system debate." It was fueled by two historical trends. First, in capitalist countries there was the concentration of capital and the formation of huge trusts and monopolies, which had replaced competitive capitalism, based largely on family-owned firms. As firms amassed economic and political power it became ever more obvious that the workhorse of much of marginalist economics—the model of perfect competition in which none of the agents possesses any market power—could not capture the new situation. Second, with the Russian Revolution of 1917, the establishment of the Soviet Union, and the growing strength of socialist parties in Europe and beyond, the contours of an alternative to capitalism gradually took shape. According to its advocates, this new socioeconomic system shed the injustices and deficiencies of capitalism and paved the way to a new world without exploitation of people, economic crises, and imperialist wars. No doubt, the profession of economists had to form an opinion on these challenges.

Here we deal briefly with the debate about alternative economic systems and their respective merits and demerits, as they were seen at the time. Chapter 7 is then devoted to a summary account of attempts to come to grips with market forms other than perfect competition.

It is interesting to note that vis-à-vis the socialist challenge several economists reacted by shoring up their defense and study of the capitalist system but continued to take their bearings exclusively from the static efficiency properties of an economy characterized by perfect competition. How much economists at the beginning of the twentieth century were entrenched in such thinking is also reflected by the fact that even a number of advocates of the socialist alternative saw the case of perfect competition as the ideal state. They differed from the defenders of contemporary capitalism only in so far as they insisted (1) that the latter was fundamentally different from the ideal and (2) that socialism, as conceived by them, showed the way back toward the ideal by means of a judicious choice of social institutions and policies. Without much of an exaggeration one could say that in this view socialism was designed to mimic the properties of competitive capitalism without private property in the means of production.

However, some authors insisted that both the defense of capitalism as well as the advocacy of socialism under consideration could not be sustained, because they shared the same deficiency: they started from a highly misleading view of capitalism. As Joseph A. Schumpeter maintained in his book *Theory of Economic Development* (first published in German in 1912), the static efficiency properties of perfect competition, around which the arguments of both parties in the controversy revolved, were of little importance for an understanding of the working of the capitalist system (both its bright and dark sides). The most striking features of capitalism, Schumpeter insisted, were its inherent dynamism and restlessness and its capacity to propel the system forward to rising levels of productivity and to an increasing variety of goods. In this regard, Schumpeter, who was not a Marxist, acknowledged that he benefited greatly from Marx's perspective (as will become more clear in chap. 8).

"MARKET SOCIALISM" Let us now briefly summarize the debate about socialism, which is also known as the "socialist calculation debate." In principle, according to Pareto, an efficient allocation of scarce resources is also imaginable in socialism. He doubted, however, that this was possible without markets—how would one recognize shortages, for instance, without the signal of rising prices? Without prices performing the function of signaling, Pareto argued, a planned economy is just groping around in the dark. This applied also to the formation of wages, salaries, rents, interest, and so on. However, if income and performance are decoupled, he concluded, there is an incentive problem: Why should anybody try hard and make an effort, if this is not rewarded properly? In a paper first published in Italian in 1908 and then in an English translation entitled "The Ministry of Production in a Collectivist State," the Italian economist Enrico Barone (1859–1924) picked up on Pareto's reflections and theorized that a socialist economy could achieve efficiency if it made conditions of static efficiency the guiding principle of its hypothetical "Ministry of Production." In his mathematical model of a socialist economy prices must reflect relative scarcities of goods and resources for a "maximum collective welfare" to obtain. Barone was clear that it was difficult first to ascertain and then to bring about such a state, not least because of the enormous amounts of data that would have to be collected and the huge computing capacity needed to process the data. Yet impressive progress made in these two regards in the decades that followed his publication made the problems look as if they could eventually be managed for good.

Ludwig von Mises, in a paper published in 1920 and then in an English translation entitled "Economic Calculation in the Socialist Commonwealth" in 1935, objected to this view by asserting that economic efficiency and individual freedom are inextricably linked to each other—without market prices there can be no rational planning. The problem was not just a lack of data or of computing capacity but went much deeper. Mises went so far as to argue that all human rationality arises out of economic life and needs the medium of markets to evolve.

The Polish economist Oskar Lange (1904–1965), who taught in the United States, answered Mises in a paper entitled "On the Economic Theory of Socialism" published in two installments in 1936 and 1937. In his view, the alternative between competitive capitalism and socialism no longer really existed, since the former had long since ceased to be. Capitalism's attributes of efficiency can only be restored, Lange maintained, within the framework of a decentralized or "market socialism." In this system the central planning authority fixes prices. If at the given prices there is excess supply on a market, the price is lowered for the ensuing period; if there is excess demand, it is increased. Via a process of trial and error that brings to mind Walras's *tâtonnement*, prices are taken to move step-by-step in the direction of a market-clearing level. Market socialism was thus posited as a successful way to realize efficiency in consumption and production.

The American economist Abba P. Lerner (1905–1982) continued the discussion, paying special attention to the Pareto optimality of market socialism. At the time, this vein of argument was met with widespread agreement—not least owing to the successes of the Soviet war economy and its notable record of economic development after the war. But "Austrian" economists in particular, much of whose reasoning revolves around the role of incomplete information and knowledge and uncertainty in the economic process, remained unconvinced.

THE MARKET PROCESS AS A DISCOVERY PROCEDURE Mises's position was supported by his fellow Austrian Friedrich August von Hayek in several writings, including *The Road to Serfdom* (1944) and essays about the role of knowledge in society. Hayek highlighted two crucial aspects of the market process: first, the incentives for microeconomic action that come from the market, and second, the information that markets generate. Prices, as the outcome of spontaneous actions by individuals, are carriers of information. Fragmented and dispersed knowledge that is only privately available is bundled into prices and thus made generally available. No central planning office and no bureaucratic process, Hayek insisted, can collect, process, and pass on information nearly as effectively as the market can. The market therefore entails a "discovery procedure." Hayek also echoed Mises in contending that economic and political freedom are intimately linked.

A "THIRD WAY"? Before, and alongside, the systems debate there was an intensive discussion, especially in German-speaking countries, about a new economic and social order—a "third way" beyond capitalism and socialism. This was triggered by the defeat of the Central Powers in the First World War (1914–1918) and the upheavals (and related economic and social miseries) caused by the war. Emil Lederer (1882–1939), a member of the German Socialization Commission along with Hilferding, Schumpeter, and others, advocated socializing "key industries" (coal, iron, steel) and instituting a governmental planning framework as a means to stabilize the economy and bring about a less unequal distribution of income. Otto Neurath (1882–1945) argued that central planning did not need prices but could instead do with a "calculation in kind" of the type used in the war economy. Carl Landauer (1891–1983) pleaded for the gradual transformation of the economy into socialist forms of organization and expected a rapid increase in economic rationality and efficiency to result. The religious socialist Eduard Heimann (1889–1967) placed the community above the individual and had confidence in the power of social welfare policy to transform the system. A decade before Lange, he had advocated the concept of market socialism.

Some of these ideas found their way into the platforms of political parties, especially those of the Social Democratic Party and the Christian Democrats, but they lost influence with the rise to power of the National Socialist German Workers' Party (NSDAP) under Hitler in 1933. During the Nazi period (1933–1945), with Germany and its allies' conquest of large parts of continental Europe, hundreds of mostly German-speaking economists and other scientists of great renown were forced to emigrate for racial or political reasons, and if they did not do so in good time they ran the risk of being sent to "concentration camps." This resulted in a tremendous brain drain out of Germany, Austria, and Nazi-occupied countries—and a corresponding brain gain of countries willing to accept the émigré scholars, especially the United States and Great Britain but also, for example, Turkey. The Rockefeller Foundation helped many scholars who had been dismissed from their universities to find positions abroad and supported the New School for Social Research in New York City, whose graduate school began in 1933 as the "University in Exile" under its president Alvin Johnson (1874–1971) to provide a haven for scholars threatened by the Nazis.

It was only after the Second World War that intellectual life and the social sciences in Germany, Austria, and other European countries recovered, but the harm done by Hitler and his cohorts left a permanent trace on the profession and fundamentally altered the academic landscape, with some American universities ascending swiftly to top positions in the field of economics and related disciplines.

The search for alternatives to capitalism or for ways to correct and tame it has not died—see, for example, works of the American economists John E. Roemer (b. 1945) and Joseph Stiglitz. The recent crisis of the financial markets and the banking sector along with the powerful impact of that crisis on the real economy raised further questions about the conditions for a world that is more stable and more just.

7
IMPERFECT COMPETITION

That a market economy, if left to its own devices, yields optimal social outcomes in conditions of perfect competition is an idea that gained a strong following among economists and is still prevalent in much of mainstream economics. In these circles Smith's warnings about the "wretched spirit of monopoly" that never rests seem to have been forgotten in spite of developments in the real world that cannot be overlooked. Other thinkers have situated themselves in opposition to this perfect competition lens, criticizing their "free market" colleagues for entertaining a sometimes naïve gullibility about the efficiency of markets and for ignoring the highly restrictive conditions under which this purported optimality applies. And indeed, it is all too obvious that capital has become concentrated, oligopolies and monopolies have formed, stock companies and the concomitant separation of ownership (by shareholders) from control (by managers) have become more important, and large conglomerates are influencing governments and the state ("trustified capitalism," as Schumpeter called it). Economics could not permanently shut itself off from the new reality, and so we see various attempts, coming from different schools of thought, to come to grips with market forms other than perfect competition. A brief summary account of some of them follows.

OLD INSTITUTIONAL ECONOMICS We begin with a quick look at what is nowadays known as "old institutional economics," which is rooted in an empirical and historical orientation and advocates an evolutionist outlook on economic phenomena; there is a clear line of continuity connecting it to the older German historical school. ("New institutional economics" instead studies social norms, organizational arrangements, and the like from the viewpoint of the neoclassical model of rational choice; see chap. 12.) Its advocates do not argue by way of constructing models but rather more sociologically. They reject the figure of *homo economicus* and the two central concepts of neoclassical economics: the concept of rationality, in the (narrow) sense of optimizing under given and known constraints, and the concept of equilibrium. In their view, David Hume's picture of people as "but a heap of contradictions"—as the playthings of passions, instincts, and habits—is closer to reality than that of the coolly calculating automaton that is perfectly informed, foresees all possible circumstances in the world, and acts optimally. The view that man fully understands the world is totally alien to institutional economists, who see institutions as a way to cope with incomplete information and uncertainty.

Perhaps the most important representative of this trend was Thorstein Veblen (1857–1929). In *The Theory of the Leisure Class* (1899), he identified social recognition and prestige as the chief motives of human action. Wealth and a high income are a means to the end of "conspicuous consumption": the public display of wealth in order to impress others is reminiscent of Adam Smith's "parade of riches." And like Smith, Veblen argued that the demand for status goods increases along with their price—the more expensive, the better. This is the so-called Veblen effect. But when markets noticeably serve individuals' vanity, how should efficiency be assessed? In his *Theory of Business Enterprise* (1904), Veblen extended his critical view to the business world. Managers and bankers chiefly follow their own interests and not those of owners and clients—and they frequently understand amazingly little about business. Their focus is very often on restricting competition and attaining monopoly rents.

John Maurice Clark (1884–1963) built upon Veblen's work, disputing the kind of consumer sovereignty assumed by neoclassical economics. As he wrote in a paper for the *Journal of Political Economy*, in 1918, "Economic wants for particular objects are manufactured out of [the] simple and elemental raw material [of primitive instincts] just as truly as rubber heels, tennis balls, fountain pens, and automobile tires are manufactured out of the same crude rubber. The wheels of industry grind out both kinds of products. In a single business establishment one department furnishes the desires which the other departments are to satisfy." And even an economist like Frank H. Knight (1885–1972), who was typically considered a leading representative of the mainstream, lamented in his 1934 essay "Social science and the political trend" the "persuasive influence by sellers upon buyers and a general excessive tendency to produce wants for goods rather than goods for the satisfaction of wants." But if demand is systematically influenced by suppliers, then supply and demand are no longer independent of each other, and the explanatory value of a theory (including of a welfare theory) whose fundamental axiom is the autonomy of agents is called into question.

Institutional economics spawned a number of other fields and concepts. For example, John R. Commons (1862–1945), in his book *Legal Foundations of Capitalism* (1924), studied the interrelationships between the economy and the legal system, focusing attention on the importance of property rights, the development of common law, the behavior of legislatures and courts, and the evolution of organizational forms. He was convinced that the driving forces of socioeconomic development are conflicting interests within the economy and society—especially the conflict between labor and capital—and the way these are resolved in different legal frameworks. He saw the government as playing the important role of a mediator between different groups and contemplated, for example, ways and means to create and enforce a "right to employment." In *Institutional Economics: Its Place in Political Economy* (1934) Commons laid out in two volumes the questions asked, the methods employed and the results obtained by institutional economics and compared it with alternative approaches. Against methodological individualism he argued: "Instead of isolated individuals in a state of nature they are always participants in transactions, . . . citizens of an institution that lived before them and will live after them," and spoke of agents possessing "institutionalized minds." Commons is considered to be one of the founders of the law and economics field.

The American economists Adolf A. Berle (1895–1971) and Gardiner Means (1896–1988) published in 1932 *The Modern Corporation and Private Property*, in which they analyzed the rise of big business in the United

States, especially from a legal point of view. They showed that U.S. corporate law was co-responsible for the separation of ownership and control and the principal-agent problem that came with it. Their book is considered one of the foundational works on corporate governance and institutional economics.

Wesley Clair Mitchell (1874–1948), a student of Veblen's, conducted mainly research into business cycles—at the time seen as one of the major problems to be understood and fought by a judicious use of economic policy instruments; see his *Business Cycles and Their Causes* (1913). Mitchell was convinced that an explanation of business cycles must not start from ad hoc and dubious psychological axioms but from empirical facts and recurrent patterns of business prosperity, crisis, depression, and revival. What was needed first and foremost was to observe, analyze, and systematize the phenomena under consideration. In Mitchell's view business cycles were endogenous to capitalism, reflecting its internal dynamism. Similar views had been put forward by Arthur Spiethoff (1873–1957) in Germany, with whom Mitchell was in close contact, and by Schumpeter in his *The Theory of Economic Development* (see chap. 8). Mitchell was one of the founders and long-term research directors of the National Bureau of Economic Research (founded in 1920)—a model for many other economics research institutes.

We now turn to developments in economic theory dealing with imperfect and monopolistic forms of competition.

MONOPOLISTIC COMPETITION In his 1926 article "The Laws of Returns Under Competitive Conditions," Sraffa drew the attention to the fact that the widespread assumption of perfect competition was empirically untenable. He insisted that firms differ from one another along a number of dimensions, including product quality, packaging, service, and location, and are in fact keen to differentiate themselves from their competitors by operating on these dimensions. In this way they seek to gain some monopoly position. The consequence is that a firm does not lose all its customers immediately if it increases the price of a product a little, nor does it corner the entire market if it lowers the price a bit, as the theory of perfect competition assumes. Within limits the firm can set the price without being driven out of the market. While the model of perfect competition assumes that firms have no economic power whatsoever and therefore are bound to accept the price of the product in the market as it is (that is, they are "price takers"), models of monopolistic competition conceive firms as possessed of a larger or smaller capacity to fix prices—they are thus "price makers." (If in perfect competition all firms are price takers, the question of how the price in the market is determined remains unanswered.)

Sraffa's 1926 article heralded the development of the theory of monopolistic competition. Harold Hotelling (1895–1973), in his 1929 paper "Stability in Competition," focused attention on one such dimension: the location of firms in space. Taking the spatial dimension of economic activity seriously lends immediate support to the thesis of monopolistic elements in competition, because firms cannot but assume different geographical positions. (We encounter a version of this again in chap. 12 in David Starrett's criticism of the competitive mechanism postulated in general equilibrium theory.) Hotelling stressed that greater spatial proximity to customers grants firms a preferential competitive edge. However, he also saw reason to argue that in well-specified conditions it is rational for firms to differentiate their products as little as possible. The case he had in mind is two shops competing along a main street of given length of a city, with customers spread uniformly along the main street. If both shops can choose their location they will settle next to each other halfway along main street. The result of minimum product differentiation is also known as "Hotelling's law." However, changing the assumptions leads one quickly to cases in which firms have strong incentives to differentiate their products and settle at a larger or smaller distance from other firms to reduce the competitive pressure to which they are exposed.

In *The Theory of Monopolistic Competition* (1933), the American economist Edward Chamberlin (1899–1967) picked up the threads of this argument and posited that firms in a market do not create completely identical products but close substitutes instead. Hence, they are monopolists to a certain degree. To what degree depends on how strongly the demand for their product reacts to changes in price—that is, how flat or steep the firm-specific demand curve is. Firms obey the monopolistic rule of profit maximization (marginal revenue = marginal cost). Through product differentiation, they attempt to increase their market power. That same year, the British economist Joan Robinson published *The Economics of Imperfect Competition*. She studied in particular the case of price discrimination. A monopolist who can sell his product on several separate markets will call for different prices, and each of these prices will obey the profit-maximizing rule of the monopolist in the respective market. The less elastically demand reacts to price changes in a given market, the higher will be the price the firm sets there.

OLIGOPOLISTIC COMPETITION As these theories of monopoly developed, attention turned increasingly to the case of oligopolies—a small number of suppliers in a given market. The focus here is on strategic behavior: when a firm changes the price of its product, it has to reckon with its competitors reacting to this change, which in turn can cause a change in behavior for the first firm, and so on. Does this process lead to a stable constellation or to equilibrium, or does it degenerate into a ruinous struggle?

This was not the first time economists had considered such a question. The French economist Joseph-Louis-François Bertrand (1822–1900), in a review of Antoine-Augustin Cournot's 1838 book *Recherches sur les principes mathématiques de la théórie des richesses*, criticized the latter's treatment of the case of duopoly (two suppliers). Cournot had based his argument on the assumption that the two firms act strategically, with each trying to anticipate how the other will respond to its competitor's decisions. Given the firms' expectations they decide simultaneously and independently of each other the quantities to bring to the market. Their output decisions affect the price they obtain in the market. If their expectations happen to be correct, profit-maximizing behavior leads to a price that is larger than marginal cost and thus larger than the price in conditions of perfect competition. Bertrand objected that if firms, instead of deciding on quantities, decide on prices, while buyers decide on the quantities they wish to buy at these prices, the result will be very different: with homogeneous products buyers will only buy from the firm with the lowest price, forcing the other firm to reduce its price. The final outcome is that firms will bid down the price until it is equal to marginal cost, which is, of course, the solution in conditions of perfect competition. In this case firms make no profits (above and beyond the normal rate of return on the capital invested), which is somewhat paradoxical, given the fact that they do have market power. Firms could, of course, *collude* and behave like a monopoly would, charging a price at which marginal revenue equals marginal cost and divide the market among themselves. There are indeed strong incentives to do so.

In his book *Marktform und Gleichgewicht* (*Market Structure and Equilibrium*) (1934) the German economist Heinrich von Stackelberg (1905–1946) treated the two duopolists in asymmetric fashion: one "leads," the other "follows." The follower maximizes his profit for a given supply of the leader. The latter, instead, maximizes his profit for a given adjustment of the other to this supply. Output and profit of the leader are, in equilibrium, greater than those of the competitor. Should both firms contest the leadership role, however, there will not be any equilibrium. There is rather the danger of a ruinous rivalry between the firms, in which both legal and illegal methods are applied. Stackelberg regarded this case as the most probable and arrived at the conclusion that equilibrium theory is ultimately of little use. In light of the oligopolization he observed, he began to doubt the capacity of the market economy to function smoothly and use resources optimally. (This was one of the reasons why he leaned for a while toward the Nazis, who promoted government-controlled cartels and a corporatist state.)

FURTHER DEVELOPMENTS Since these early works on imperfect and monopolistic competition a rich literature on various market forms has evolved and has given rise to a new field of economics known as "industrial economics" or "industrial organization." An integral part of it is a theory of the firm, the firm's boundaries, and its relationship with the market. The questions asked are, in particular: Why are there firms (that is, nonmarket institutions characterized by hierarchies among members) whereas in markets agents are formally equal? Why are not all economic transactions directly mediated via markets? In "The Nature of the Firm," published in 1937, Ronald Coase (1910–2013) argued that firms exist because they allow one to economize on transaction costs, such as costs of negotiating, of writing enforceable contracts, and soon. He also pointed out that—because of uncertainty clouding economic activities—labor contracts, especially, are necessarily incomplete. Within limits the boss can expect employees to execute his orders, even though the tasks involved have not been specified in any detail in the labor contract.

Coase's neoclassical explanation did not pass unchallenged. A huge managerial and behavioral literature evolved, some of it derived from Herbert Simon's observation that in complex and uncertain situations agents can only exercise "bounded rationality": instead of optimizing they are "satisficing," that is, they set themselves attainable goals and are satisfied when these are achieved. In several contributions the idea that the firm is a monolithic entity has been refuted. In the literature on the principal-agent problem it is argued that managers (agents) typically try to pursue their own interests to the detriment of the principal (shareholder) and are within limits able to do so, because the principal cannot directly observe the agent's actions or could do so only at prohibitively high monitoring costs.

The American mathematician John Forbes Nash (1928–2015) developed noncooperative game theory to deal with the strategic interaction of several agents or firms. A "Nash equilibrium" is a solution of a noncooperative game in which each agent is supposed to know the equilibrium strategies of all other agents and cannot improve his situation by altering his own strategy. The outcome of the game cannot be predicted by looking only at a single agent in isolation, because the agent can be assumed to make his decisions by trying to take into account the decisions made by all the others. Noncooperative game theory and the concept of the Nash equilibrium have been applied to a wide range of situations characterized by conflicts of interest, such as oligopolistic competition, arms races, and war (see also chap. 12).

In addition to the theoretical side of industrial organization, there is an applied and descriptive one dealing with the actual organization of companies and industries and their development over time. See, for example, Joe Bain's (1912–1991) *Industrial Organization: A Treatise* (1959), Alfred Chandler's (1918–2007) *The Managerial Revolution in American Business* (1962), and Frederic Scherer's (b. 1932) *Industrial Market Structure and Economic Performance* (1970). In the respective literature important themes are the advantages of mass production and, more generally, the economies of scale and scope. Whereas in the case of scale the firm's efficiency increases with the quantity of the product it produces (due to increasing returns that are internal to the firm), in the case of scope it increases with the variety of products it produces. This is because of the indivisibility of some input, learning processes, and the recurrent application of proprietary and tacit know-how. Hence product diversification may improve a firm's performance.

Finally, industrial economics deals with the policy issues of economic regulation, antitrust law, patent law, and all aspects of industrial policy, including R&D.

8

SCHUMPETER AND THE PRINCIPLE OF CREATIVE DESTRUCTION

"Innovation is the outstanding fact in the economic history of capitalist society," writes Schumpeter in his *Theory of Economic Development* (1912). "Innovations" he defined as "carrying out new combinations" in the economy and society—developing new products, improving product quality and production methods, conquering new sales markets, and reorganizing firms and entire industries. As with Smith and Marx, Schumpeter was concerned with understanding capitalism as a "cultural phenomenon" encompassing all spheres of life—economic, social, political, juridical, religious, and artistic—and its "law of motion," a term he borrowed from Marx. It deserves to be mentioned in passing that Schumpeter was probably one of the best-read economists ever, which is impressively documented in his huge tome *History of Economic Analysis* (1954), published posthumously. It contains a treasure trove for all interested in the history of the subject from its very beginning up until the mid-twentieth century.

How does capitalism, Schumpeter asked, create of its own accord the energy that moves it incessantly? What is its internal logic and why is it bound to undergo, over time, a process of self-transformation? What are the causes of its restlessness? These are the themes he tackled, first in his *Theory*, then in his monumental *Business Cycles: A Theoretical, Historical, and Statistical Analysis of the Capitalist Process*, published in 1939. In these works he located the main source of capitalism's inherent dynamism in the economic sphere, from which change radiated to the other spheres and was reflected back to it. What had to be understood was the interdependence of the spheres—their coevolution. Schumpeter therefore supplemented his economic analysis with one of the modern political system in terms of a theory of democracy and of the long-term trend of capitalism in a later and highly successful book, *Capitalism, Socialism, and Democracy* (1942). He accused all previous economists, excepting Marx, of ignoring the most important feature of capitalism: its dynamism. The received static models of conventional economics, revolving around the concept of equilibrium, were unable to capture this feature: "Development and equilibrium are mutually exclusive."

CREATIVE DESTRUCTION In classical economics and in Marx, the source of dynamism is systemic: the "coercive law of competition," in Marx's words, drives the system's development. Economic competition means rivalry, and in that rivalry only those who innovate or who at least imitate successfully survive in the market. New economically useful knowledge—manifested in new goods, new methods of production, new organizations of business—is frequently the enemy of old knowledge, that is, knowledge is not always cumulative. The process is one of "creative destruction"—Schumpeter's famous term describing the Janus-faced nature of development. Technological change incessantly revolutionizes the entire economic system, bringing new goods, firms, and professions into being and taking old ones out of service. It forces profound changes on society and has both winners and losers. Harmonious progress is not its business.

For Schumpeter, the deeper source of this dynamism is the action of the "entrepreneur." Although he cherished the achievements of Walrasian theory, he objected that it knows only "static," "hedonic," and "rationalistic" types who conform to prevailing circumstances. In this perspective agents are concerned with adjusting as best as they can to prevailing conditions: they optimize, subject to given constraints. They are "boring equilibrium men" as far as Schumpeter is concerned. A completely different type of agent, entirely overlooked by conventional economics, is the "dynamic" and "energetic" agent—the entrepreneur—and his "creative response." He does not accept the circumstances as he finds them, does not arrange himself with given conditions—he is rather intent on overcoming them, on pulling down the obstacles he encounters, and on adding new dimensions to economic activity. Not everyone is capable of this. People who have the requisite imagination, willpower, and tolerance for risk constitute an "elite," are "chieftains" in the economic world. Schumpeter was full of admiration for these people, because in his view they are the yeast in the dough of society and propel the system forward. But he also saw some dark sides of these personalities. "Such men create because they cannot help but do it." They aspire to a "position of social power" and rejoice in "victories over others." Schumpeter even pointed out how "half-pathological moments" must be enlisted to explain some entrepreneurs' behavior. They are workaholics and often have little taste for the pleasures of life. Yet entrepreneurs are the key players in the drama of creative destruction, and to understand capitalism one has to understand their role in it.

INVENTION, INNOVATION, IMITATION Schumpeter distinguished among invention, innovation, and imitation. Inventions, he stressed, are economically irrelevant unless they survive the test of the market, gain economic weight, and so turn into innovations. Not everything that represents new knowledge is also economically valuable. The entrepreneur is typically not also the inventor, but someone who has the talent to select from the stream of inventions those that can be profitably marketed. Inventors do not usually have this capacity, as they focus on technical aspects to the detriment of economic ones.

Innovations can, but need not, yield abnormally high profits. If they do, these are transitory: "They are both the child and the victim of development." The typical diffusion process of new economic knowledge illustrates this. When an invention becomes an innovation, the "first act of the drama" unfolds—its introduction into the economic system. The successful entrepreneur is an agent of change who breaks the "static spell," opens up new economic spaces, and paves the way for followers. The pioneer may at first reap high "monopoly profits." Higher profitability allows the pioneering firm to grow faster than its competitors. Via differential rates of growth of firms, the new knowledge embodied in new goods, new methods of production, and so on gains in importance relative to the old one.

But the diffusion process is considerably accelerated only in the "second act of the drama," which has two phases. In the first phase, firms following "the impulse of enticing profits" of the first mover try to imitate the innovator and copy its new device. This leads to an increase in the level of output of the commodity under consideration and an intensification of competition among the firms producing it. In the example of a new method of production that allows for a reduction in unit costs, sooner or later the price of the product will be bid down toward the lower production costs. This ushers in the second phase, since now all static firms are getting into trouble. Producing so far with relatively low profits, they are now incurring losses. In "fear of total annihilation" they are forced to modernize their firms, production techniques, and work routines. A growing swarm of firms tries to resist their extinction by imitation. Not all will survive. The drama resounds with "the cries of the crushed over which the wheels of the new go."

With the diffusion and generalization of the new, competitors will gradually catch up with the pioneering firm and undermine its monopoly position. As a consequence, "the profits of the entrepreneur and also his entrepreneurial function as such perish in the whirlpool of the competitors that are at his heels." The system moves in the direction of a new "circular flow," a stationary state of the economy, in which the "law of cost" is reinstated and the prices of commodities are again equal to their costs of production. Because of the increase in productivity entailed by innovations, the incomes of the broad masses are now higher than in the old state. This is Schumpeter's version of the doctrine of the unintended consequences of self-interested behavior, which we encountered in Adam Smith. The selfish behavior and need for achievement of the few causes, behind their backs so to speak, an increase in the wealth of the many.

The process is "evolutionary" and knows no end, Schumpeter stressed: in the wings the enemy of the new is already lurking, waiting to be the one who will soon supersede the last innovation.

LONG WAVES OF ECONOMIC DEVELOPMENT According to Schumpeter, the process is discontinuous and cyclical. In *Business Cycles* we read: "Cycles are not, like tonsils, separable things that might be treated by themselves, but are, like the beat of the heart, of the essence of the organism that displays them." The notion that it is possible to have a cycle-free capitalism—advocated only recently by economists ranging from Robert Lucas (b. 1937) to former Federal Reserve chair Ben Bernanke (b. 1953)—is

something Schumpeter can safely be assumed to have received with disbelief and amusement. Factual developments have, in any event, cast a harsh
light on the naïveté of this view—recall, for example, the talk about the
"Great Moderation," meaning the alleged demise of the business cycle, followed by what was called the "Great Recession" in recent years.

Schumpeter was in agreement with Arthur Spiethoff, his fatherly friend
and colleague, according to whom in each phase the business cycle offers
strong incentives: in a boom there is "the carrot of profits," and in a slump
"the stick of distress." In principle, Schumpeter was convinced there is no
boom without innovation and no downturn without exhausting its potential. Schumpeter regarded as misguided from the outset any purely monetary explanation of crises and business cycles that puts the blame on the
banks and their policy of easy money, as offered, for instance, by Hayek in
his book *Prices and Production* (1931), and does not take innovations and
creative destruction into account.

While Schumpeter, drawing on the work of business cycle researcher
Clément Juglar (1819–1905), initially estimated cycles to be about nine to
ten years long, he later added the concept of the "long wave," which spans
approximately fifty years. Business cycles made an appearance during the
Industrial Revolution around the 1820s, when the manufacturing sector
had gained sufficient importance relative to agriculture and was organized
on a capitalist basis. Prior to that only agricultural cycles of good and bad
harvests were known—recall the seven good years of corn and the seven
thin years in the Bible. As regards long waves, Schumpeter followed the
Russian statistician Nikolai Kondratieff (1892–1938) and Spiethoff, who
had discerned in the statistics on prices, wages, interest rates, and other magnitudes available to them long upward trends followed by downward trends
of economic activity. While Kondratieff had focused attention on nominal
magnitudes, Schumpeter drew the attention to long waves in real variables:
output as a whole and outputs of particular sectors of the economy, labor
employment, the capital stock in the economy. For the period up through
the First World War, Schumpeter discerned three long waves, each of which
was triggered by technological breakthroughs affecting the entire system,
later called "basic innovations": the so-called first Kondratieff was triggered
by the steam engine (1787–1842), the second by the railway (1843–1897),
and the third by electrification (1897 until ca. 1940). A fourth Kondratieff

was later associated with the automobile and a fifth with information and communications technology.

CREDIT AND BANKS In a stationary economy—Schumpeter's "circular flow of economic life"—in which the same production and consumption processes take place day in and day out, money's only function is as a medium of exchange. It lies like a veil over the real economy but does not exercise any influence on it. But in a dynamic, innovating economy, things are different. Implementing new combinations requires withdrawing productive resources from old combinations—used by incumbent firms—and passing these resources on to the innovator. But the innovator is typically without wherewithal and thus dependent on bank credit. (Schumpeter actually also discussed other forms of financing investment, including venture capital, but the emphasis was on bank credit.) It is in the best interest of the banks that lend the innovator money to form a solid judgment on the profitability of the proposed project. This calls for thorough expertise and a long-term orientation on the part of the banks, because very often it takes a long time for a novelty to become known and to sell.

Credit is the lever of a withdrawal of resources on behalf of the innovator. In an economy in which all productive resources are fully employed, an increase in the overall demand in monetary terms leads to an increase in the prices of productive resources. The inflation induced by credit expansion can be compared with a tax on static firms, and channels needed resources into the hands of the entrepreneur. According to Schumpeter it is only now that "capital," "profits," and "interest" enter the arena. Capital consists exclusively of the purchasing power handed over to innovators. It is not itself productive, but a precondition to be met for productivity increases to obtain. Neither produced means of production nor accumulated savings are capital, as received theory contends. Capital, rather, is credit given to new producers. Schumpeter therefore speaks of his "purchasing power theory of capital." For a process of development to take off, he maintained, no prior savings are needed. It suffices to give credit to the innovator. Only as a consequence of innovations will savings result from realized profits and increases in other kinds of income.

Schumpeter called the money or credit market the "headquarters of the capitalist economy." Interest is a deduction from profits and is paid for the provision of liquidity. Capital, profits, and interest exist only in a dynamic economy not in the circular flow—a view with which he challenged basically all existing theories, classical, Marxist, marginalist (neoclassical), or Austrian.

Schumpeter saw the banking system as on the one hand providing the needed additional liquidity to realize innovations that increase the quantity and quality of goods available in the economy. On the other hand he observed that the banking system was prone to overshooting and fueling speculative bubbles, which after bursting deepen and prolong economic crises that necessarily follow upon the absorption of the new combination into the economic system. Like Adam Smith and many other economists before him he called for judicious regulation and control of the banking sector.

SCHUMPETER'S LEGACY Schumpeter's ideas have fallen on fertile ground in many fields of the social sciences. They have been taken up in business economics and especially by the management literature on entrepreneurship. Schumpeter is also considered one of the founding fathers of "evolutionary economics," in which economic development is understood as a process of selection whose creative side increases variety, whereas its destructive side decreases it. At issue is the complexity of the process of innovation and the best way to capture its salient features. The founding work is *An Evolutionary Theory of Economic Change* (1982) by Richard Nelson (b. 1930) and Sidney Winter (b. 1935); see also *Evolutionary Economics and Creative Destruction* (1998) by Stanley Metcalfe (b. 1946). Other important representatives of evolutionary economics include the German Ulrich Witt (b. 1946) and the Italian Giovanni Dosi (b. 1953).

In what is frequently called "new growth theory" there is one branch that formalizes some of Schumpeter's ideas within a largely neoclassical framework; see in particular the book by Philippe Aghion (b. 1956) and Peter Howitt (b. 1946), *Endogenous Growth Theory* (1998). The main purpose of this kind of literature is to explain technological progress as generated from within the economic system.

The concept of basic innovations can be said to recur in a paper by Timothy Bresnahan (b. 1953) and Manuel Trajtenberg (b. 1950) titled "General purpose technologies: 'engines of growth?'" (1995). General purpose technologies exhibit the following three characteristic features: (1) they are pervasive, that is, they affect large parts of the economic system; (2) they offer a large scope for further improvements; and (3) they exhibit substantial innovative complementarities between the industry supplying the technology and those using it (forward and backward linkages).

In the 1970s, the Schumpeter student and Keynesian Hyman Minsky (1919–1996) developed a theory of the "instability of financial markets." At the beginning of a cycle, according to Minsky, investors practice "hedge finance": from out of their earnings they can pay back not only interest but also loans. As the boom progresses, the investors' willingness to assume risk grows, and they move on to "speculative finance": now they can only service their interest payments while they replace old credits that come due with new ones. The last stage is called "Ponzi finance," named after the operator of a fraudulent snowball system. In the often exuberant expectation that they can still pocket large profits in the end, investors even borrow on credit to pay off interest debt. Risk increases by leaps and bounds until the speculation bubble pops.

Schumpeter had a major influence in sociology and political science. His *Capitalism, Socialism, and Democracy*, which expresses his vision of the unity of the social sciences, is still on the reading list of many courses taught in these disciplines. Widely discussed was his conviction that because of the trend toward monopolization and bureaucratization, the law of motion of capitalism involves its transformation into some form of socialism. His analysis (using tools and arguments forged in economics) of the political process in democracies, in which political parties compete for the votes of the electorate, sparked off a huge literature on alternative voting systems and their implications.

We now turn to a man of comparable learnedness and a greatly influential public figure in the first half of the twentieth century with whom Schumpeter competed in vain for the title of the most important economist of his time. The scholar under consideration is, of course, John Maynard Keynes.

9
KEYNES AND THE PRINCIPLE
OF EFFECTIVE DEMAND

Arguably the most influential economist of the twentieth century was John Maynard Keynes, who taught in Cambridge, England. He is significant not just for his writings but also for his activity as an adviser on economic policy and a member of various delegations for the British government (especially for the Treasury) in international negotiations. Economists, according to his credo, should contribute to improving the human condition: "If economists could manage to get themselves thought of as humble, competent people, on a level with dentists, that would be splendid!" In light of the world economic crisis that erupted in 1929, acting smart about economic policy was a matter of necessity. An enlightened liberal who wanted to preserve the capitalist order based on a market economy, Keynes believed that only government intervention and regulation could protect the system from destroying itself.

MACRO THEORY AND MACRO POLICY Running through Keynes's entire work is a concern for economic policy guided by reason and a longing for a more productive and equitable society. In 1919 he published *The Economic Consequences of the Peace*, which was informed by his role in the peace negotiations at Versailles in the aftermath of World War I and which became an immediate best seller worldwide. In the book, Keynes articulated his dismay at the reparations imposed on a vanquished Germany, arguing that it would be impossible for Germany to raise the amount of resources required as "reparation payments" and that the effort to do so would not only impair economic activity in Germany but throughout Europe. In this way, the victorious powers would be shooting themselves in the foot. His prediction came true. Germany could not meet the requests, economic activity in Germany dwindled and unemployment rose. Imports shrank, which reduced sales abroad, and worst of all, the deteriorating economic conditions paved the way for the rise of Hitler and the Nazis.

In his *Tract on Monetary Reform* (1923), Keynes turned to the problem of reforming the monetary system and revealed an impressive degree of practical knowledge about financial markets. (Indeed, along with his junior colleagues Richard Kahn and Piero Sraffa, he dealt successfully on the stock market.)

In his 1930 *Treatise on Money*, he presented a macroeconomic analysis of national income, employment, and money, building on Knut Wicksell's *Interest and Prices* (1898) and radicalizing some of that earlier work's ideas. He argued, for instance, that there is no reason to assume that an economic system left to its own devices will tend toward the full employment of labor. But even with this work, Keynes still did not really overcome the "received doctrine" and was not capable of explaining the world economic crisis and proposing measures to fight it. There was an urgent need for a general theory that explained both the functioning of the economic system and its failure to function—which Keynes attempted in 1936 with the publication of his *General Theory of Employment, Interest and Money*.

Many ideas contained in his magnum opus are not new in themselves but in their combinations. Before we embark on illustrating this it deserves to be mentioned that in important respects Keynes was anticipated by the Polish economist Michal Kalecki (1899–1970) in several essays published beginning in 1933, initially in Polish and only later translated into English, which made them accessible to a broader readership. There is no indication that Keynes was influenced by Kalecki. The latter, just like Keynes, argued that the level of investment determines national income and savings, which makes investments basically self-financing—as Kalecki famously stated, "Capitalists earn what they spend, workers spend what they earn." A high level of investment leads, via a high level of effective demand, to high profits. Kalecki's supposition here is that the concentration of market power (which hardly plays much of a role for Keynes) is reflected in a macroeconomic "degree of monopoly" that determines the share of profits in national income. Throughout his life Kalecki remained in Keynes's shadow, undeservedly so in light of his pathbreaking work.

THE CRITIQUE OF ORTHODOXY *The General Theory* took aim at Say's law in its neoclassical version and especially at the thesis that unemployment is merely a result of real wages that are too high. (Keynes himself spoke of "classical theory," but neoclassical is what he really meant. He did not always show a firm knowledge of the history of economic thought.) In wage negotiations, it is only the money or nominal wage that is at issue, not the real wage, which reflects the actual purchasing power of wages vis-à-vis the price level of commodities (that is, the money wage divided by that price level). The effects of a falling nominal wage must be considered in their economy-wide context, insisted Keynes—something partial equilibrium analysis of the labor market fails to do. According to Keynes, falling wages of workers will first and foremost reduce the demand for consumer goods, which results in sinking consumer goods prices (on the assumption of price flexibility). But if wages and prices fall broadly parallel to each other, the real wage remains approximately constant and the mechanism on which neoclassical theory relies does not apply.

During the Great Depression, prices and wages in the United Kingdom did indeed fall together; the real wage even rose slightly! What is more, as demand fell and the rate of capacity utilization of plant and equipment declined, there was no incentive for businesses to invest: Why add to the existing productive capacity in view of its falling rate of utilization? Since aggregate demand in an economy is equal to the sum of consumer and investment demand (if, for simplicity's sake, we omit all government activity and foreign trade), Keynes concluded that aggregate demand will fall along with wages. This leads to additional job dismissals and a worsening of the situation—just the opposite of what the neoclassical economists contended.

According to Keynes two other factors come into play when wages and then prices fall. In anticipation of commodity prices falling even further, demand may fall. More important, falling prices worsen the situation faced by debtors (frequently businesses), because the real value of their debt increases. A debtors' crisis ensues, in which firms become insolvent and go bankrupt. This then has a detrimental effect on debt holders, and the result is a crisis of confidence of creditors in borrowers. The economic system is in peril of self-accelerating destabilization (so-called debt deflation). The remedy prescribed by neoclassical economic policy—cutting wages in order to increase employment—worsens rather than improves the situation. Numerous historical illustrations, including the Great Depression, substantiate Keynes's finding. Conventional neoclassical theory is said to suffer from a "fallacy of composition": results that have been derived within a partial equilibrium framework do not necessarily carry over to the economic system—the whole is not just the sum of its parts. If the system is not self-equilibrating at full employment, there is not only room but the need for economic policy that accomplishes what the economy when left to itself does not accomplish. The policy Keynes suggested was designed to stimulate and stabilize aggregate effective demand by means of monetary and fiscal measures (low money rates of interest, an increase in public expenditures, lower taxes, etc.).

THE PRINCIPLE OF EFFECTIVE DEMAND Let us now have a closer look at Keynes's view that the economic system is typically not fully utilizing its productive resources—it is not "supply-constrained," as neoclassical economists contend, but "demand-constrained" (except during booms). More specifically, Keynes's "principle of effective demand" means that there is no reason to assume that aggregate investment demand will always be large enough to employ all of an economy's productive resources. To see this we must turn to how he determined the two components of private domestic aggregate effective demand—consumption and investment expenditures.

Before doing so, it should be noted that Keynes conceived savings (correctly) as the nondemand of goods and services. The saver keeps a part of his or her money income and does not spend it, that is, does not buy goods. Savings in themselves involve "leakages" in the stream of expenditures and pose the problem of sufficient effective demand. The praise Adam Smith had showered upon the "frugal man" was justified only to the extent to which the saver was at the same time an investor, who spent the saved sums not on consumption goods (food, beverages, clothing, etc.) but instead on investment goods (plant and equipment, raw materials, etc.). In this per-spective investments involve "injections" into the stream of expenditures and may compensate for the leakages stemming from savings.

In what he called a "fundamental psychological law," Keynes stated that aggregate consumption expenditure (C) depends first and foremost on the level of national income (Y): the larger the latter, the larger also the former. Consumers are not the active agents in the economic system, investors are. Consumers tend to be passive, reacting to changes in national income. In the simplest case of a linear consumption function, we have $C = cY$, with c representing the propensity to consume. (Keynes assumed a slightly dif-ferent consumption function, in which the propensity to consume was not a constant but decreased as national income increased, but this need not concern us here.) With $c = 0.8$ or 80 percent (meaning that 80 cents of each dollar earned are spent on consumption), a total income of $100 billion yields a total consumption expenditure of $80 billion. Since sav-ings (S) equal income minus consumption, $S = Y - C$, the savings function that corresponds to the above consumption function is given by $S = sY$, with s representing the propensity to save or savings rate. Obviously, the percentage of income that is not consumed will be saved, which means, of course, that $s = 1 - c$. So from our example above, $1 - 0.8 = 0.2$ or 20 per-cent. Savings out of a total income of $100 billion would accordingly be $20 billion. Hence, both consumption expenditures and savings increase (or decrease) when national income increases (or decreases). At a total income of $200 billion, consumption expenditures would be $160 billion and savings $40 billion.

Consumption and savings depend first and foremost on the level of national income, but what decides the latter? This is the crucial ques-tion. Keynes answered: it is the level of investment demand. Investors, not consumers (alias savers), are the active element in the economic system. Whoever invests today generates a larger capital stock and thus a larger productive capacity in the hope and expectation that the larger output that can be produced tomorrow and thereafter will be absorbed by the market and yields higher profits. The investors operate their way into an uncer-tain future. Since they cannot have reliable information about that future, they must base their decisions to invest on long-term expectations about future economic situations. Depending on whether they are optimistic or pessimistic—Keynes famously described the emotions and instincts of investors as "animal spirits"—they will invest either more or less.

The important point to note here is that while consumption expenditures are decided dominantly on the basis of an economic magnitude (national income) describing the actual state of the economy (a "state variable"), investment expenditures depend dominantly on magnitudes that cannot be known as yet: the investors cannot *know* the future and whether their investments will be profitable or not. They cannot know the prices of commodities in the future, the wage rates they will then have to pay to workers, the increase in technical knowledge that might make their investments technologically obsolete, and so on. They cannot even base their decisions on a probability calculus, because they do not know the probabilities with which different outcomes of their investment activities occur. In terms of a distinction suggested by Frank Knight, investors are not simply confronted with risk but with fundamental uncertainty. They must base their decisions to invest on long-term profitability expectations.

THE MULTIPLIER Let us assume that, as an expression of investors' long-term expectations about profitability, there is an aggregate investment demand (I) of $10 billion. This demand leads to an income of $10 billion in the industries building investment goods (machines, tools, construction, etc.). Of this income, 20 percent ($2 billion) is saved, but 80 percent ($8 billion) is used by its recipients (workers, capitalists, etc.) to buy consumer goods. We therefore arrive at an income of $8 billion in the consumer goods–producing industries (food, beverages, cars, etc.). Of this income, in turn, 20 percent ($1.6 billion) is saved and 80 percent ($6.4 billion) consumed, which leads to an additional demand for consumer goods and therefore to additional income, expenditures, and so on. The investment demand thus triggers a process of income generation and expenditure that ultimately leads to a national income ($10 billion + $8 billion + $6.4 billion + $5.12 billion + . . .) from which just as much is saved ($2 billion + $1.6 billion + $1.28 billion + $1.024 billion + . . .) as was invested, namely $10 billion. For $s = 0.2$, the resulting national income is equal to $50 billion. In general, $Y = (1/s)I$.

The expression $1/s$ is the so-called multiplier—equal to 5 in the example above. Keynes borrowed the idea from Richard Kahn, a member of the "Cambridge Circus" that supported him with critical advice as he developed his *Treatise on Money* and *The General Theory*. (The idea itself, though, is older; first soundings of it can be traced back to the physiocrats.) The multiplier "translates" a certain level of investment and the effective aggregate demand it stimulates into the corresponding national income. What applies to absolute magnitudes applies also to changes (denoted by Δ) in the magnitude. Let us assume that investments increase by $1 billion ($\Delta I = \$1$ billion). This would then produce an increase in national income of $5 billion ($\Delta Y = \$5$ billion) and additional savings at the level of the additional investment ($\Delta S = s\Delta Y = \Delta I = \$1$ billion). If investment activity fluctuates, then national income, consumption, and savings also fluctuate. Business cycles are closely tied to fluctuations in investment activity. Keynes's central message is this: *It is not savings that determine investments, but investments that determine savings.* Savers do not determine the course of events, but rather investors! The economic policy conclusion that follows from this is that overall investment has to be stabilized at a level equal to savings obtaining at the full employment level of national income.

INTEREST, MONEY, AND EMPLOYMENT While the above argument contains the thrust of Keynes's reasoning regarding the relationship between investment and savings and arguably his most innovative contribution with respect to received neoclassical theory, it is not the full story. Keynes repeatedly deplored the difficulty of "escaping received modes of thought," and his concept of the determinants of investment demand is a case in point. While he emphasized the importance of long-term profitability expectations, he also saw that the money rate of interest exerted some influence. Firms that cannot finance all their investments by means of retained profits made in the past need additional liquidity. One way to get it is to take a loan from a bank, and the interest the bank charges is a cost the firm incurs that reduces its profits. (There is also the following consideration: a firm with retained profits faces among other things the alternative of investing them into an expansion of its productive capacity or of bringing it to the bank and earning interest. The higher the interest rate the smaller the incentive to invest.) Keynes incorporated this element into his analysis entirely in the same way as it is done in neoclassical theory: the higher the interest rate i, the higher the cost of financing investment, and thus the smaller is I; correspondingly, the lower the rate of interest, the larger the volume of investment. But when investors react to lower interest rates with an expansion of investment activity, the decisive question is: Can i fall to a level at which I then becomes large enough for full employment, and can we rely on it falling to that level?

According to Keynes, this is possible but very unlikely. The main reason is a high "liquidity preference"—a "love of money"—that prevents the interest rate from falling as far as would be necessary. Money, Keynes argued, is basically required for two reasons: as a medium of exchange when buying and selling goods (money is thus needed because of the "transaction motive") and as a store of value to guard, as best as possible, against the uncertainty clouding the future (money being held because of the "speculative motive"). This makes money attractive to agents. Yet if liquidity preference is high, the price for parting with it is also high, and this price is nothing else than the money rate of interest.

This is another distinguishing feature of Keynes's theory as compared with neoclassical theory: while in the latter the interest rate is taken to be the magnitude that equilibrates savings and investment (at full employment), in Keynes it equilibrates the demand for and the supply of money or liquidity. The upshot of Keynes's argument is that if liquidity preference is high (and can even be expected to increase as societies become richer) the interest rate cannot be expected to fall to so low a level that the volume of the corresponding investment engenders the full employment of labor.

This brings us to a third difference between Keynesian and neoclassical economics. In the latter money serves essentially only as a means of exchange and not as a store of value, and so does not affect the real economy in a substantial way. Money has therefore been called a "veil" that covers the real system; it can be removed without much effect on the latter. Things are quite different in Keynes's analysis, in which the real and the monetary sphere of the economy are intimately intertwined. The root of the interdependence of the two spheres, as Keynes saw it, is that money serves also as a store of value. Obviously, if this role becomes more important in a particular historical situation, agents will keep larger cash balances (they will hoard money), which means that expenditures will be reduced. This affects the real economy, because firms can now sell less and might, as a consequence, dismiss workers, and so on.

Keynes elucidated his idea of why keeping money need not be irrational by using the example of a special asset, a so-called consol, with a fixed interest payment per year and an infinite maturity. Whoever owns this kind of security has a claim to an annual interest payment at a given level (let us say $100) from now to eternity. While the annual amount of interest is fixed, the share price of this tradable security is variable. The higher its price, the lower the security's effective interest rate, which equals the ratio of the fixed interest payment to the price of the asset. If the price is abnormally high, many financial investors will expect it to fall, which would imply a potential loss to them. If the loss due to an expected fall in the price of the asset is larger than the annual interest yield, they will prefer to hold money instead of the asset. For a given overall money supply of the central bank, the aggregate demand for money can now be so large that the money rate of interest is well above the rate that is compatible with full employment investment. The system gets stuck in an "unemployment equilibrium."

Keynes was convinced that this is the normal state of affairs in highly developed, rich economies. He offered three reasons in its support. First, in accordance with the "fundamental psychological law," savings do not (as previously assumed here for simplicity's sake) grow in proportion to income, but more than in proportion. That is, the propensity to save (s) increases with an increase in income per capita, so the potential deficiency of effective demand tends to get larger. (This trend, as Keynes and especially Nicholas Kaldor [1908–1986] argued, is amplified by a redistribution from wages to profits, because the propensity to save out of profits is greater than the propensity to save out of wages. Such a redistribution has taken place on a global scale during the recent past, as Tony Atkinson and Thomas Piketty have documented in several studies.)

Second, and simultaneously, Keynes, again following in the footsteps of conventional neoclassical economics, saw a worsening of profit expectations with respect to real capital formation: to the degree that capital becomes more "abundant" in a given country, it becomes less "scarce" relative to labor, and as a consequence the expected rate of return on capital tends to decrease. As a result, the *propensity* to invest declines.

Third, a money rate of interest that is relatively rigid downward because of the liquidity preference of the public—people willing to hold cash balances—prevents the *ability* to invest to improve. The high cost of getting the needed liquidity dampens investment. The system is caught in a dilemma: the propensity to invest declines, but it would be essential that it increase to counteract the depressive tendency arising from an increase in the propensity to save and an insufficient downward flexibility of the money rate of interest. In a developed economy, Keynes opined, there are strong stagnation tendencies at work as a result of these three factors. They can only be overcome by skillful monetary and fiscal policy, the stabilization of business expectations, and (in extremis) investment controls.

THE "KEYNESIAN REVOLUTION" The Keynesian message (or what was taken for it) swiftly conquered the academic and also parts of the economic policy world. Contributing to its success were books by Alvin Hansen (1887–1975) and especially Paul A. Samuelson's textbook, *Economics: An Introductory Analysis*, first published in 1948 and translated into several languages. The deep economic depression of the 1930s and the inability of conventional theory to explain and provide prescriptions for overcoming the crisis nurtured the impression that economics was in a profound crisis. Keynes pointed the way to a much-needed reorientation. As Milton Friedman and then-president Nixon famously exclaimed: "We are all Keynesians now!"

Not only did *The General Theory* trigger important developments in economic theory, such as establishing macroeconomics and dynamic economic theory as new fields; it also brought about the further development of national income accounting and its international harmonization, especially by Richard Stone (1913–1991), as well as of empirical economic and business cycle research. Already in 1930 the Econometric Society had been founded, at the instigation of the Norwegian economist Ragnar Frisch (1895–1973), as an organization dedicated to formulating economic theories mathematically and testing these theories with statistical methods. Keynesian income and expenditure models were now scrutinized econometrically, initially for individual countries and then later for several countries trading with one another.

Public finance experienced a reorientation at the hands of Richard Musgrave (1910–2007), who took up the Keynesian message in his tripartition of the subject. In an influential textbook published in 1959 he distinguished among three types of government functions: allocation, distribution, and now also stabilization. He argued that the government should be concerned with providing high levels of employment and growth and a socially desirable distribution of income and wealth by using Keynesian effective demand management and incomes policy.

The Keynesian message did indeed revolutionize economic policy. Its core concept was the management of aggregate income and expenditures by means of economic policy instruments that exerted an influence on domestic investment demand, domestic consumer demand, public expenditure, and exports—so-called injections—on the one hand, and domestic savings, taxes and exports—so-called leakages—on the other hand. Anticyclical monetary and fiscal policies were designed to mitigate business cycles and lead to high rates of employment, a stable price level, a balanced foreign trade, and steady growth. In economic downturns the monetary authorities were advised to reduce interest rates and the government to increase public expenditures, reduce taxes, and thus run a budget deficit, whereas in booms the interest rates should be increased, public expenditures reduced, and taxes raised, implying a budget surplus. The idea was that in this way the volatility of economic activity would be reduced and grave losses in employment and output as a whole avoided. Over a succession of (mitigated) booms and slumps, budget deficits and surpluses were supposed to cancel, so that from the point of view of stabilizing the economy, a balanced budget was obtained on average. (Budget deficits were allowed if they were due to public investments in a country's infrastructure [roads, rivers, ports, etc.], the education and health system, and the like.) High levels of employment and capacity utilization, a stable price level, balanced trade, and steady economic growth became enshrined as policy goals. The success or failure of governments was measured in terms of whether and to what extent they succeeded in realizing these goals.

While, as we shall see below, Keynesianism went out of fashion in the 1970s, some of its basic ideas stood the test of time. Governments engaged in fierce anti-Keynesian rhetoric nevertheless ran ever-larger budget deficits to finance, for example, wars. And with the most recent financial crisis, which set loose the specter of a global financial meltdown, some variant of Keynesianism became fashionable again in several countries, including the United States. The biographer of Keynes, Robert Skidelsky (b. 1939), summed it up in the title of one of his books: *The Return of the Master.*

10
REACTIONS TO KEYNES

Keynes's work won over many converts—but what exactly does "Keynesianism" mean? Great works leave ample room for alternative interpretations, especially when, like *The General Theory*, they feature some blurriness, limitations, and weaknesses.

THE LONG RUN Keynes's analysis was deliberately restricted to the short run. That is, he was concerned with ascertaining the level of employment and output as a whole at a given place and time and did not investigate in detail the forces that affected the movement of these magnitudes over time. In other words, he focused attention only on a single effect of investment demand, which we may call the "income or effective demand effect of investment." As we saw in chapter 9, he described this effect by means of the multiplier. However, investment has at least two further important effects that Keynes was aware of but treated only in passing. First, net investment I adds to the capital stock of the economy, K, that is, $I = \Delta K$, and thus increases the economy's productive capacity or potential output. We can call this the "capacity effect of investment." Second, gross investment is one of the vehicles by which new economic knowledge enters the economic system—new and better machines, computers, and so on. (The other vehicle is "human capital"—that is, better-educated, skilled labor.) We can call this the "productivity-enhancing effect of investment."

The first two effects bring up the question: If investment activity governs both the development of effective demand and that of potential output over time, which path would investment activity have to follow for the two developments to continually match, so that any increase in productive capacity is always accompanied by an increase in effective demand of the same magnitude? In this case the growing capital stock would always be fully utilized, because effective demand would develop in harmony with potential output.

Evsey Domar (1914–1997) and Roy Harrod (1900–1978) studied this problem in the late 1930s and 1940s; see especially Harrod's *Towards a Dynamic Economics* (1948). Imagine that net investment, year after year, remains constant. In this case effective demand, given by the multiplier, would also remain the same over time. However, the capital stock would increase every year by $I = \Delta K$ and together with it productive capacity. A constant level of effective demand and an ever-rising level of potential output imply an ever-decreasing degree of capacity utilization. Obviously, this would not be a sustainable situation. In order for the income and capacity effect to balance, and therefore for macroeconomic demand to keep pace with the expansion of productive capacity, investments need to grow over time and to do so at a very specific rate that Harrod called "warranted." It is "warranted" in that it guarantees that investors' expectations will be fulfilled: they have expanded their productive capacity in the expectation of growing markets, and actual developments bear them out.

What happens if investments do not grow at the warranted rate? If they grow faster, demand will grow more rapidly than productive capacity, and capacity utilization will increase. If investors (wrongly) conclude that they were not optimistic enough as to the expected growth of markets and expand their investments more swiftly, they only expand the discrepancy between the income and capacity effects: the system runs into a boom. In the opposite case, the capacity effect surpasses the income effect, and the system slides into a cumulative downward trend—a depression. In both cases, equilibrium is perched precariously "on the razor's edge": deviations from the warranted rate are amplified. (Harrod did not see things to be so rigid as the notion of a razor's edge suggests; he rather had in mind a corridor outside of which instability obtains.) This is Harrod's "instability theorem": the economy transmits signals that can easily be misunderstood and trigger reactions that worsen the situation instead of improving it. The system might fail to self-regulate and needs to be stabilized by judicious economic policy measures.

ECONOMIC GROWTH AND PUBLIC DEBT If the state intervenes for this and other purposes (infrastructure, education and science, national defense, etc.) and finances some of its activities not via taxes but via public debt, the question of how large a public debt the economy can cope with arises. In a paper published in 1946, Domar dealt with this problem within the framework of a steadily growing economy. Domar emphasized that in assessing public debt, it is not its absolute level that is crucial but the ratio of that level to the GDP—the government debt ratio. The situation becomes unsustainable when the latter is rising over time. This is the case when the real rate of interest to be paid on the debt (the nominal rate minus the expected increase in the price level) exceeds the growth rate of real GDP and that of taxes. A growing public debt in absolute terms, Domar concluded, is perfectly compatible with a constant or even falling debt ratio, and the growing interest burden will not, in the given circumstances, devour the growing tax revenues.

Some people are inclined to believe that public debt is per se bad and dangerous and must be fought at all cost. This naïve view cannot be sustained. Adam Smith and economists both before and after him have identified cases that justify the debt financing of certain public expenditures that provide an array of public goods, such as roads, schooling, national defense, and many more. The need to stabilize the modern economy indicates an additional case not anticipated by Smith, who was dealing with an economy that was in important respects very different from the one we live in today. Domar delineated in abstract terms the confines within which a public debt is sustainable.

CYCLE AND TREND Many contributions were devoted to the relationship between economic cycles and the long-term trend of the economy. This problem had already been tackled by Kalecki, who had argued that the trend or long-term development of the economy is nothing but the result of the sequence of short-term constellations through which it passes. In the 1930s, picking up on Marx and Mikhail Tugan-Baranowsky

(1865–1919) rather than Keynes, Kalecki developed several models to explain both the cyclical character of development and the growth trend. These are compiled in his *Essays in the Theory of Economic Fluctuations* (1939). In the following year he published his essay "Political Business Cycle," in which he argued that a successful employment policy will make labor more scarce and thus cause wages to increase—resulting in growing resistance from employers that ultimately leads to the abandonment of the policy. He insisted that permanent full employment and capitalism are incompatible with each other.

If economic activity is cyclical, that is, upswings are followed by downswings, what explains the reversals, the upper and the lower turning points? According to Kalecki, the boom runs up against the "full-employment barrier," whereby wages, prices, and interest rates are driven up and the profitability of capital formation diminishes, increasing the risk for credit-financed investments. With rising national income and rising domestic prices, imports increase and exports decrease. This can lead to balance of payment problems. The boom is broken and the economy experiences a downturn. In a slump, wages, prices, and interest rates will fall, tending to improve profitability and international competitiveness.

MULTIPLIER AND ACCELERATOR In a paper published in 1939 Paul A. Samuelson formalized the problem of cycle and trend in terms of what is known as the "multiplier-accelerator model." In it he linked the idea of the multiplier with that of the accelerator—referring to an investment function in which net investment today is assumed to depend on (or be induced by) a change in effective demand, that is, the difference between output actually demanded in the present period and realized output in the previous period. If effective demand has increased, then the level of investment picks up, whereas when it has decreased, investment will slacken. Depending on how strongly investment reacts to such changes in demand (measured by the so-called accelerator coefficient) on the one hand, and the magnitude of the propensity to save on the other, Samuelson showed that over time the system can behave very differently. He provided a typology of possible cases, which include steady growth, cycles with constant amplitudes, but also contracting or exploding cycles. Changing one of the parameters (the accelerator coefficient or the savings propensity) may push the system from one regime into another. That is, it may affect the behavior of the system not only quantitatively but also qualitatively. This goes against the continuity assumption entertained in much of economic analysis, in which there is no room for such regime changes. Recall the motto of Alfred Marshall's *Principles of Economics* (1890): "natura non facit saltum"—nature does not make jumps. However, in his book *Industry and Trade* (1919), apparently under the influence of recent developments in physics (especially quantum physics), he backed away from this statement and postulated instead "natura abhorret saltum"—nature abhors jumps—which is an altogether different claim.

AUTONOMOUS INVESTMENT In 1950 John Hicks published his *Contribution to the Theory of the Trade Cycle*. The upper turning point of a cycle—when a boom ends in a crisis, which triggers the downturn—can be easily explained (as it was by Kalecki) in terms of a "ceiling" hit by the economy (full employment of labor, excess capacity utilization, rising wages, and falling profits). However, it is less clear what is responsible for the lower turning point, the "bottom" below which economic activity cannot fall even without a stabilization policy implemented by the monetary authorities and the government. The main reason for this, said Hicks, was that investment is not only "induced" by changes in demand for given products (as in Harrod) but is partly "autonomous" in the sense that it does not depend on demand in given markets but is caused by expectations regarding demand in emerging markets. In short, by means of autonomous investment new goods and new methods and means of production are channeled into the economy. Information about current state variables of the system has only limited meaning for the success of these investments. A turnaround may also be due to so-called automatic stabilizers. Institutions like unemployment benefits and social insurance prevent consumption from falling below a certain level. Finally, declining costs may improve the international competitiveness of domestic firms and lead to rising exports.

IS-LM **MODEL AND THE NEOCLASSICAL SYNTHESIS** The majority of contributions dealt with up until now were concerned with extending Keynes's analysis to the long run and thus with overcoming one of its important lacunae (another being its limitation to a closed economy, setting aside foreign trade and capital movements). At the same time a huge industry sprang up providing alternative interpretations and criticisms of *The General Theory*. It should not come as a surprise that major representatives of what was then mainstream economics would seek to understand the message of *The General Theory* within the analytical framework to which they were accustomed. In his influential paper "Mr. Keynes and the 'Classics'" (1937)—the reference is to the neoclassical economists—John Hicks reinterpreted *The General Theory* in Walrasian general equilibrium terms and elaborated the so-called *IS-LM* model. This model became the workhorse of macroeconomics for decades and some version of it is still popular today.

A characteristic feature of attempts to look at Keynes through the lens of neoclassical theory is that unemployment is traced back to rigidities in the system. These prevent the system from functioning smoothly and effectively. Rigidities concern especially the wage rate, the prices of goods, and the interest rate. Without such rigidities, it is contended, the economic system would bring about a tendency toward the full employment of labor and the full utilization of the capital stock. (This does not mean that there is no room for economic policy, because the adjustment process of the private enterprise economy to such a state of affairs may be slow and could be accelerated by state interventions.) The theoretical focus in this literature was therefore on the causes and effects of such rigidities, and the economic policy focus was on how to remove such rigidities or outmaneuver them.

Hicks condensed the Keynesian message (or what he understood it to be) into a model with two markets—the goods and the money market. The gist of his reinterpretation consisted in the construction of two relationships. One reflects all possible equilibria on the goods market, characterized by an equality between savings (S) and investment (I); the other reflects all possible equilibria on the money market, characterized by an equilibrium between the demand for liquidity (L) and the central bank's supply of money (M). The former relationship is known as the *IS* curve and the latter as the *LM* curve.

The first relationship describes the combination of all levels of national income (Y) and the interest rate (i) at which planned savings (S) equal planned investments (I). In accordance with Keynes, the higher the national income, the higher the savings, while investments are assumed to be higher the lower the interest rate is. Thus the *IS* curve exhibits an inverse relationship between Y and i that guarantees the equality of I and S and an equilibrium on the market for goods.

The second relationship relates to the monetary side and indicates all combinations of Y and i at which the demand for money or liquidity (L)—meaning the sum of the money demand from the transaction and from the speculative motive—equals the money supply (M) provided by the central bank. The relationship between Y and i here is positive: the higher the national income, the higher is the money demand from the transaction motive. In order for the money demand from the speculative motive to be equal to the remaining money supply, the interest rate must rise along with national income. This is the so-called LM curve: along this curve, equilibrium prevails on the money market.

The intersection of the IS and LM curve, finally, determines the level of Y and i at which both markets are in equilibrium (see fig. 10.1). The economic system is said to gravitate toward this equilibrium. In this view, the level of effective demand (investment plus consumption) decides the level of employment. If investment is slack, then total effective demand is slack; correspondingly, labor employment will be low. If investment is brisk, demand is brisk, and labor employment is high. Unemployment is not a "disequilibrium" phenomenon, because it can be expected to prevail due to the rigidities contemplated in the model, especially an insufficient

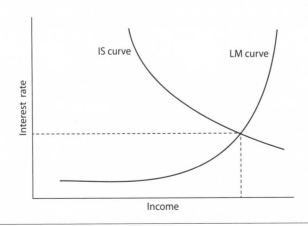

FIGURE 10.1 The IS-LM model

downward flexibility of the interest rate, an investment demand that does not respond much to a change in the interest rate, and a possibly high liquidity preference.

Franco Modigliani (1918–2003) was the first to integrate a labor market into the model in his paper "Liquidity preference and the theory of interest and money" (1944). This rendered complete what Samuelson called the "neoclassical synthesis," which reformulated certain Keynesian ideas within a neoclassical analytical framework. The neoclassical case of full employment and the Keynesian one of unemployment thus emerge as the result of different constellations of the parameters defining the underlying behavioral relationships with regard to investment, saving, and liquidity preference. On the one hand the neoclassical case is characterized by an investment demand that is highly elastic with regard to the level of the rate of interest and a demand for money that is not interest-elastic, meaning that the speculative motive (and thus the function of money as a store of value) plays no role. Hence investment can be expected to attain a level compatible with full employment savings. On the other hand there is the Keynesian case, in which investment is not very sensitive to changes in the interest rate, but the demand for money is very interest-elastic, and at the extreme even infinitely elastic: just a small decline in the interest rate leads to a robust expansion in the demand for cash. This is the so-called liquidity trap. In this case the interest rate is prevented from falling very much, and even if it did, investment would not be stimulated much: dull long-term profitability expectations paralyze the economy. The system finds itself in an "unemployment equilibrium." (A notable example of very high liquidity preference associated with economic stagnation, which has now lasted for more than two decades, is the case of Japan.)

This analysis has important implications for the effectiveness of both monetary and fiscal policies. An expansive monetary policy, in which the central bank increases the money supply through the purchase of government bonds on the open market, and which shifts the *LM* curve to the right, does not produce any appreciable decline in the interest rate and therefore cannot stimulate investment enough to bring about full employment. In such a situation only an expansionary fiscal policy promises any remedy by shifting the *IS* curve to the right. (The experience in the United States, Europe, and Japan after the recent financial crisis has shown that

Keynes's fear of a downward rigidity of the interest rate [above the zero bound] was not justified—in fact not only the real but in some countries even the nominal rate of interest turned negative. At the same time it has proved Keynes right that in such a situation monetary policy is of little use and fiscal policy has to step in.)

Interestingly, Keynes's response to Hicks's formalization was moderately positive, but many of his followers rejected it. Joan Robinson called it "bastard Keynesianism," contending that it forced Keynes's original thoughts into the Procrustean bed of the conventional equilibrium logic and thus robbed them of their revolutionary character. The inherent instability of the system and the role of uncertainty and fluctuating expectations were left out. These factors play an important role in post-Keynesian theory.

POST-KEYNESIAN THEORY Exponents of this orientation in economics agree that neoclassical re-interpretations of Keynes are misleading and cannot be sustained. They agree much less on the essence of Keynes's message and how it should be developed and applied in policy recommendations. This is understandable, especially because, as Pierangelo Garegnani (1933–2011) remarked, *The General Theory* represents an "unsound compromise" between entirely novel elements (such as the multiplier) and conventional ones (such as an investment function that is elastic with regard to the rate of interest). Some of the most important representatives of post-Keynesianism are the Cambridge (UK) economists Joan Robinson and the Hungarian-born Nicholas Kaldor, the Italian economist Luigi Pasinetti (b. 1930), the British economist George Shackle (1903–1992), and the American economists Hyman Minsky and Paul Davidson (b. 1930). What unites the post-Keynesians is their rejection of the following neoclassical tenets: Say's law and the assertion of a tendency toward full employment; the idea that money is draped like a "veil" over the real economy, on which it has no influence; the thesis that savings determine investment rather than the other way round; and the marginal productivity theory of income distribution.

Robinson and Kaldor put forth post-Keynesian theories of capital accumulation and income distribution. In their contributions, published in the mid-1950s, they started from the assumption of full employment on the ground that Keynesian effective demand management was working well. Kaldor's model, especially, became very prominent. He stressed that it was based essentially on an application of the multiplier to the long run. While the working of the Keynesian multiplier presupposes (fairly) constant prices but variable quantities (because outputs can adjust vis-à-vis idle productive resources without causing prices to rise), in a fully employed economy quantities are (fairly) constant in the short run, but prices are variable. With money wages that are also constant, an increase in the share of investment in national income (I/Y), and thus an increase in the rate of capital accumulation (I/K), implies a larger effective aggregate demand that results in a rising price level. With prices rising relative to money wages, real wages will fall and profits (P) increase. An increase in the share of profits (P/Y), in view of a fairly constant capital-to-output ratio (K/Y) representing what Kaldor called a "stylized fact," means the rate of profits (P/K) is bound to rise, since $P/K = (P/Y)(Y/K)$. The redistribution of income away from wages to profits is the mechanism that, according to Kaldor, brings about the adjustment of the overall share of savings in national income (S/Y) to the increased share of investment (I/Y), because the propensity to save out of profits is typically larger than the propensity to save out of wages. (Kaldor considered firms' retained profits to be an important part of savings out of profits.)

Kaldor's model illustrates anew the Keynesian message that investments lead to savings of the same magnitude and not the other way round, but this time the mechanism is different—it is not via an adjustment in quantities, given prices, real wages, and the distribution of income, but via an adjustment in prices and the distribution of income, given quantities. Kaldor's model also sees income distribution to be determined not by the marginal productivities of the factors of production but rather by the factors affecting the speed at which capital accumulates.

The post-Keynesian approach to the problem of income distribution in a world in which all productive resources are fully utilized met with the following objection: in conditions of full employment, workers and trade unions are strong and should be able to negotiate higher money wages vis-à-vis a rising price level. This would, however, thwart the mechanism by means of which income distribution and a fortiori the overall propensity to save adjust to changing conditions of capital accumulation.

In several papers published in the 1960s and 1970s, Kaldor crossbred Adam Smith's concept of the division of labor and Keynes's principle of effective demand. He argued that with an expanding division of labor, returns to scale increase dynamically. Especially the size of the manufacturing sector matters, because it proved to be an "engine of growth." When Great Britain acquired a competitive edge in the world markets as a consequence of the Industrial Revolution, foreign demand accelerated the growth of the manufacturing sector, which, in turn, amplified its leading role. Here we are confronted with a virtuous circle, in which a climate of brisk effective demand is conducive to the exploitation of increasing returns. According to Kaldor, conventional neoclassical equilibrium theory cannot deal with the important case under consideration, because there is no equilibrium or rest point of the economy. The economy, rather, is constantly in motion. Its development is "path dependent" (meaning that whatever has happened in the past has an irreversible impact on the present) and almost impossible to predict, since even small historical events can noticeably influence the course of things.

The interplay between the monetary and the real sphere of the economy assumed center stage in a number of writings. While Keynes had assumed that the monetary authorities are able to control the money supply, many post-Keynesians disagreed and argued that the money supply is endogenous—the central bank can only control the rate of interest. Paul Davidson rejected the neoclassical interpretation of Keynes championed by Hicks and Samuelson and insisted instead on the genuine novelties of *The General Theory*: money is not neutral in the sense that it typically does not affect the real variables, and closely related, produced goods that yield a positive return cannot be substituted for money. If they could, money could not constrain employment and output as a whole and Say's law would apply. Davidson insisted that many economic decisions are subject to fundamental uncertainty about future events and are not susceptible to treatment by probability theory in the way conventional risk analysis would have it. Hyman Minsky emphasized, as discussed in chapter 8, the inherent instability of the financial sector, which tends to spread out to the entire economy.

NEOCLASSICAL-KEYNESIAN SYNTHESIS The contributions that can be grouped under this name consist essentially of theoretical developments based on the neoclassical synthesis (discussed earlier) in response to newly available economic facts. Interpretations of the Keynesian message from the perspective of neoclassical theory, as has already been stressed, are united in their assertion that Keynesian economics is an economics of rigidities and does not really contain much new. (It should suffice to cast a mere fleeting glimpse into *The General Theory* to challenge this supposition.) Yet economic developments in the 1970s and the new phenomenon of "stagflation"—economic stagnation combining growing unemployment *and* inflation—amplified the critique of Keynes and nourished doubts about whether a high level of employment can be brought about without inflationary tendencies.

In the movement away from Keynes, a particular interpretation of the so-called Phillips curve established by the British economist Alban William Phillips (1914–1975) played an important role. In a 1958 paper, Phillips ascertained that, for Great Britain, there was a long-term inverse relationship between the growth of money wages and the unemployment rate (Phillips curve I). At lower rates of unemployment, employees and their trade unions would have greater negotiating power and could achieve higher wages. In a 1960 paper, however, Paul Samuelson and Robert Solow (b. 1924) gave Phillips's findings another interpretation: as a long-term stable trade-off between the inflation rate and unemployment (Phillips curve II). A constant level of prices goes along with a certain degree of unemployment, and so a high level of employment can only be achieved with higher inflation rates. In the long run, money is not neutral but affects the unemployment rate via its influence on the inflation rate. Since full employment is more important to politicians than price stability, inflation accelerates.

In a book published in 1963 the Israeli economist Don Patinkin (1922–1995) introduced Keynesian considerations into a theory of general equilibrium that he broadened to include a money and credit sector. Much of his argument revolves around the "real cash balance effect," which consists of a generalized "Pigou effect" and starts from the fact that the real value of the outside money available in the economy rises (or falls) with a falling (or rising) price level. Households, Pigou argued, will notice that this affects their wealth and as a result will expand (or restrict) their consumption. In a depression with falling prices this is a kind of automatic mechanism that guides the economy back in the direction of full employment.

The real cash balance mechanism fails, however, when prices (and wages) are rigid. In that case, the decision-making calculation of agents changes, since they will be "rationed" on one market or another. In this case it is not good enough for agents to look only at prices, as is typically assumed in neoclassical theory. They must also take into account quantity constraints they face in different markets. For example, in the labor market households might wish to sell more labor power at the given wage rate but cannot, because firms do not wish to expand production and output, as they are rationed on the goods market (that is, cannot sell more goods). Prices and wage rates no longer fulfill their traditionally intended function of balancing supply and demand, transactions will instead be based on what have been called "false prices" (that is, prices that do not clear markets), and supply or demand for some agents will not be satisfied.

Important exponents of this kind of approach were the American economist Robert Clower (1926–2011) and the Swedish economist Axel Leijonhufvud (b. 1933). The former gave us the concept of the "dual-decision hypothesis": if you are not rationed on any market, you will take only (relative) prices into consideration in your decision-making calculation. Not so if you are rationed on one or several markets (unemployment, queuing, etc.). Thus the worker who has no job will take this fact into consideration in his consumption behavior, just as sales problems of a firm affect its demand for labor and raw materials. Rationing in one market impacts on the situation in other markets and reverberates back on the original market. It is shown that this calls the quantity theory and the neutrality of money into question.

MONETARISM In reaction to some of the previously mentioned contributions, "monetarism" redefined the quantity theory of money. The Chicago economist Milton Friedman (1912–2006) in his paper "The Quantity Theory of Money—A Restatement" (1956) argued that the theory is not a theory about the effect of the money supply on the price level but rather a theory about the demand for money—or more precisely, about the demand for real cash balances. If the demand for money happens to be stable, then the price level is determined by the money supply. In another paper published in 1968 Friedman insisted that only in the short run is there a trade-off between inflation and unemployment as stipulated by the Phillips curve II. But in the long run, he insisted, there is a "*natural rate* of unemployment" that is completely independent of economic policy measures and compatible with every rate of inflation. "Natural" unemployment is voluntary—it does not express any disequilibrium but instead the preferences of employees. Unemployment can, accordingly, only be driven below the level of the natural rate when workers do not foresee the effects of rising prices on real wages and the real cash balance. If workers anticipated these effects they would react by asking for higher wages to compensate for rising prices, and employment would not be affected. While workers may be taken by surprise in the short run, in the long run they will learn to read correctly the implications of an economic policy designed to reduce unemployment. As a consequence, in the long run there is not the trade-off that Samuelson and Solow had stipulated—the Phillips curve II is a straight vertical line at the level of the natural rate of unemployment, and various levels of the inflation rate are compatible with it. An economic policy that does not understand this and seeks to reduce unemployment will only generate an accelerating inflation.

The stagflation of the 1970s was grist for Friedman's mill. He recommended an economic policy in which the central bank stabilizes inflation expectations at a low level. This requires the money supply to grow in pace with the production potential. In this way, Say's law, once pronounced dead, rose heroically from the ashes in new garb. As Keynes's colleague Dennis Robertson (1869–1963) once remarked: "If you stand in the same place long enough, the hunted hare comes round again."

NEW CLASSICAL MACROECONOMICS Following on the intertemporal equilibrium theory of Irving Fisher (1867–1947), Robert Lucas and Thomas Sargent (b. 1943), in a paper titled "After Keynesian Macroeconomics" (1979), developed a macroeconomic approach that became known as "new classical macroeconomics." It represents a stripped-down version of a general equilibrium model and starts from the following bold premises: all economic aggregates can be derived as the result of agents' rational behavior; there is perfect flexibility of all prices and factor incomes; all markets are permanently cleared; therefore all unemployment is by definition voluntary. It is clear from the outset that there is no way for this approach to capture such phenomena as involuntary unemployment and crises. "Adaptive expectations," which are formed on the basis of past experiences, are seen as incompatible with rational behavior. Rational agents are taken to be forward-looking as they maximize their profits or utility and are assumed to apply all available information about the future development of markets and economic policy measures. While single agents may make mistakes, in the aggregate these mistakes cancel each other out. On this premise, the authors feel entitled to tell their story in terms of a single representative agent only, thus setting aside all social tensions and conflicts of interest between different individuals and groups of people.

In a world like this, in which all is for the best, how could economic policy ever work, and why would it even be tried? It could only work if agents do not anticipate its effect, that is, if policy is constantly serving them up with surprises. Only then can monetary policy affect employment, though this effect is temporary at best. Rational agents will quickly understand that they have been deceived, and they will adjust their behavior accordingly. With rational expectations it is not possible to lower unemployment permanently below its natural level.

Obviously, we are facing a variant on a theme introduced by Milton Friedman. And very much like him Lucas and Sargent contended that a misguided economic policy, while incapable of permanently increasing employment, can cause a lot of damage by creating inflation and consequently increasing uncertainty. This renders the decision process of agents more difficult and error-prone. Moreover, (unproductive) government expenditures are bound to crowd out (productive) private investment—no wonder, since full employment holds sway by assumption! New classical theory buttresses the monetarist critique of the Phillips curve II and denies the curve's validity. Thus, not only does a "Keynesian policy" create no benefits; it actually inflicts damage.

In this view the malfunctioning of the economic system is first and foremost the result of interventions into the system by the state and the central bank. If left alone, the new classical economists are convinced, the private enterprise economy would work smoothly and effectively. Lucas interpreted business cycles as reflecting the reactions of economic subjects to monetary "shocks," that is, unanticipated changes in monetary policy. The impulses from such shocks lead to changes in overall economic supply, because agents initially interpret the shocks incorrectly as changes in relative prices. To this extent, therefore, money is not neutral in the short run.

The theory of real business cycles developed by Edward Prescott (b. 1940) and Finn Kydland (b. 1943) removed this residue of nonneutrality by attributing any observable fluctuations of macroeconomic aggregates exclusively to unexpected changes in technology and preferences. According to them business cycles reflected agents' optimal reactions to information that had suddenly become available.

The picture sketched here of a perfectly functioning economy and the associated frontal attack on the Keynesian message was aptly characterized by Willem Buiter (b. 1949) as "the macroeconomics of Dr. Pangloss." In Voltaire's satire *Candide ou l'optimisme* (1759), Dr. Pangloss takes the view that we live in the best of all possible worlds and that everything has been exquisitely arranged—even though catastrophes of all sorts are happening all around him and poverty and misery prevail. As a consequence of the Great Recession triggered by the recent financial crisis, new classical macroeconomics and the theory of real business cycles have lost much of their former standing in the profession. In his presidential address to the American Economic Association in 2003, Lucas had boldly contended that thanks to progress in macroeconomic theory "the central problem of depression-prevention has been solved." Had he only been right then, this would have saved many people a lot of trouble.

NEW KEYNESIAN MACROECONOMICS A new Keynesian answer to the economics of Dr. Pangloss was begun by George Akerlof (b. 1940) and Joseph Stiglitz. They analyzed the behavior of rational actors in light of price rigidities and asymmetrically distributed information, especially in the context of labor and credit markets with *im*perfect competition. With imperfect, especially oligopolistic, competition commodity prices are relatively rigid, because if one firm changes its prices, other firms will retaliate. The result may be a price war that is very costly for all firms. For fear of triggering such a debilitating war, firms keep prices constant.

A further important element of the approach of Akerlof and Stiglitz is that typically firms can only monitor their employees' performance at a prohibitively high cost, and so they avail themselves of other means to avoid shirking on the job and low labor productivity. The extra wages they pay, even in the face of unemployment, are "efficient" from the firms' point of view in the sense that the gains due to higher productivity outweigh the extra wages.

While competition for jobs between the unemployed and the employed has the effect of lowering wages in the traditional neoclassical model, this is not the case in the present perspective. The "efficiency wages" paid are profit maximizing for the firm and do not erode with involuntary unemployment. A worker who is employed and paid an efficiency wage has an incentive not to shirk, because if he or she does and this shirking is discovered he or she will pay a high price for it.

In a paper with Andrew Weiss (b. 1947) on "Credit rationing in markets with imperfect information" (1981) Stiglitz looked into the phenomenon of credit applications being rejected by banks even when those rejected included creditworthy potential borrowers. Credit rationing results when the demand for credit at the prevailing interest rate exceeds the supply of credit, and yet banks are not prepared to meet the excess demand or to raise the interest rate. This case of market failure is attributable to an asymmetric distribution of information between the principal (the bank) and the agent (the borrower). An increase of the interest rate would not only reduce the demand but according to the banks' expectations would also increase the proportion of credit applications coming from people with poor creditworthiness. The reason for this is the following. Borrowers want to finance risky projects, about which the bank has imperfect information. The higher the risk, the higher the expected profit from a project and also the higher the probability that the project will fail. Applicants with high creditworthiness and low risk would withdraw their applications when interest rates are higher, fearing they will not be able to pay back the loan plus interest. Things are different with agents willing to bear large risks: if they succeed, high profits beckon, and if they fail, the bank has to sustain the loss. This results in adverse selection, which the banks try to avoid by means of rationing credit rather than increasing the interest rate. In this way they expect to maximize profits. Credit rationing therefore is considered an equilibrium phenomenon and, as in the case of efficiency wages, has involuntary unemployment as a consequence.

BEWARE OF CHIMERICAL PROJECTORS! Adam Smith had anticipated this argument in *The Wealth of Nations* (1776). His observations read like a commentary on the recent financial crisis. With the (occasionally hypertrophic) growth of a bank's business, bankers can know "very little" about their debtors. They give money to "chimerical projectors, the draw-ers and re-drawers of circulating bills of exchange, who would employ the money in extravagant undertaking, which, with all the assistance that could be given them, they would probably never be able to compleat, and which, if they should be compleated, would never repay the expence which they had really cost." The problem, Smith stressed, is that "chimerical projectors" are willing to offer high rates of interest to banks because they expect very high profits from their "extravagant undertaking" and should the under-taking fail do not intend to pay back the debt. The "sober and frugal debt-ors," who "might have less of the grand and the marvellous, [but] more of the solid and the profitable," on the contrary, would be prepared to pay only a lower rate of interest after careful calculation. Banks can therefore be expected to go for the chimerical and not for the sober and frugal. This leads to an adverse selection, which transfers a great part of the capital of a country "from prudent and profitable, to imprudent and unprofitable undertakings."

NEW NEOCLASSICAL SYNTHESIS Among those reacting to the debate between new classical and new Keynesian economists was Michael Woodford (b. 1955) with his book *Interest and Prices* (2003). The model he presented is based (in its reduced form) on three equations. The first is a formulation for the intertemporal (that is, across time) utility-maximizing behavior of a "representative household." This representative household, an artificial agent widely used in the recent literature, is not formed by consistent aggregation across many individuals characterized by different features, but rather simply posited. It would therefore be bold to say that there is a micro foundation to this model. The second equation contains the new Keynesian version of the Phillips curve. This determines the infla-tion rate via the price-setting behavior of monopolistically competing firms. The third contains a monetary policy reaction function. As stated by this function, the central bank changes the nominal interest rate in accor-dance with the so-called Taylor rule, named after John B. Taylor (b. 1946). The Taylor rule states that the interest rate reacts both to deviations of the current inflation rate from the desired rate and to deviations of GDP from potential output. If the current inflation rate exceeds the desired rate, the central bank raises the interest rate to restrain demand. If GDP falls below potential output, the central bank lowers the interest rate to stimulate demand. The goal is to minimize inflation and deviations from potential output. Money is not neutral, but monetary policy can keep violations of neutrality within narrow limits.

The title of Woodford's book refers to Knut Wicksell's *Interest and Prices* (1898). The subject of both books, ultimately, is the question of whether the money rate of interest is or is not equal to the "natural rate" (that is, equal to the profit rate), and what happens if the former deviates from the latter. If the money rate is smaller, we get inflation, and in the reverse case we get deflation. One can say with Schumpeter that old ideas come to the ball wearing a mask. At heart, they remain largely unchanged.

II

GENERAL
EQUILIBRIUM THEORY
AND WELFARE THEORY

In the middle of the twentieth century, parallel to the rise of macroeconomic theory following Keynes, there were additional developments in the
theory of general equilibrium and in welfare economics. The Walrasian focus
on long-run equilibria was abandoned in favor of short-period equilibria,
even though (paradoxically) the time horizon of actors in some new models
was posited as infinite. One of the reasons for the turn away from the concept of long-period equilibrium, as discussed further later in this chapter, was
the difficulty of reconciling this with a given initial endowment of heterogeneous capital goods. The most important authors were John Hicks, Paul A.
Samuelson, and Kenneth Arrow, along with the French economists Maurice
Allais (1911–2010), Gérard Debreu, and Edmond Malinvaud (1923–2015).

JOHN HICKS In his book *Value and Capital* (1939), Hicks specified the
economy's initial endowment of "capital" as a set of available quantities of
different capital goods. But as Walras had already noticed, for an arbitrarily
given set of capital goods it cannot be assumed that each of them yields its
owner the same rate of return. Some such goods may, for example, be available in excess supply and thus yield no profit at all. Hicks admitted this and
tried to overcome the impasse by abandoning the traditional (classical and
neoclassical) method of long-period equilibrium, which revolves around
the concept of a uniform rate of profits in competitive conditions, in favor of

the method of short-period or "temporary" equilibrium. In a temporary equilibrium, some of the capital goods may be available in excess supply, which means that the temporary equilibrium cannot last for long. In fact, from a long-period perspective the superfluousness of some capital goods expresses a *dis*equilibrium that can be expected to lead to quick reactions on the part of economic agents. In particular, the production of capital goods that turn out to exist in excess supply will be interrupted until the stocks are run down and there is no longer an excess supply. Then production of these goods will be taken up again.

In order to determine prices, quantities, and so on in a temporary equilibrium, not only preferences, technological alternatives, and initial endowments—the usual data in general equilibrium theory—must be known. Agents' expectations about the future state of the world must also be taken as given. Since the future temporary equilibrium will typically be different from the present one, agents cannot count upon an unchanging world. Hence in each period they must form expectations about the future, and since these expectations affect agents' behavior in the present, any such temporary equilibrium depends on such expectations. Expectations are bound to change as the economic system changes over time, with each new constellation of quantities, prices, and distributive variables containing the germ to further changes. Hicks assumed that the expectations of the economic agents are given in any period of time. He thereupon specified a temporary equilibrium along with the production quantities, prices, wages, and profits associated with that equilibrium. But since a uniform profit rate is merely an accidental outcome of the resulting equilibrium, we get reactions from agents, and the game starts from scratch again. The entire development consists of a sequence of temporary equilibria, which do not, however, reveal any center of gravity toward which they are tending. The temporary equilibrium lacks any kind of persistence, which is typically the hallmark of equilibrium. Hicks later distanced himself from his own concept, convinced that it did not lead anywhere and that, crucially, depending on the assumption about expectation formation and revision the system can be taken to follow almost any path whatsoever.

PAUL A. SAMUELSON Samuelson tilled almost all the existing subfields of economics and developed new ones. His *Foundations of Economic Analysis* (1947) ushered in the age of modern mathematical economic theory, with each and every economic problem redefined as a problem of optimization (maximization or minimization) under given constraints. An important tool of the analysis became the "method of comparative statics": this amounts to comparing two equilibria, one defined in terms of a given set of data (preferences, initial endowments, technical alternatives), the other defined in terms of the same set except for a single difference. For example, how do two economies compare if they differ only in terms of the size of the workforce? The method is comparative and static, because it does not investigate how an economy would adjust over time to a new situation characterized by a larger workforce. The kind of comparison under consideration involves an analytical shortcut, because it assumes that the adjustment of the economy, triggered by a change in one datum, would converge precisely to the new equilibrium that has already been stipulated quite independently of this process. The implicit assumption is, of course, that any equilibrium is stable; that is, deviations from it would be corrected by the actions of agents. Samuelson applied this kind of analysis to, among other topics, international trade and the theory of public goods.

HECKSCHER-OHLIN-SAMUELSON TRADE THEORY In the case of the former, he fell back on the neoclassical theory of trade as developed by the Swedish economists Eli Heckscher (1879–1952) and Bertil Ohlin (1899–1979) and extended this into what became known as the Heckscher-Ohlin-Samuelson or HOS model. Assume that there are two countries (home and abroad) that exhibit different endowments of labor relative to land (the only production factors taken into account in this model). Assume also the same technological knowledge and the same preferences of agents for the two countries. Assume, finally, that both factors (labor and land) are fully employed. Before opening up trade to foreign competition, the wage rate in the home country, which has a relatively abundant endowment of labor, is lower than the wage rate abroad, because labor is relatively less scarce. As a consequence of this the prices of those goods made with relatively much labor are relatively cheaper at home. Conversely, the rent of land abroad will be smaller than at home, because land there is relatively more abundant and thus less scarce. After trade barriers are removed, the HOS model predicts that the home country specializes in the production of relatively labor-intensive goods and exports a portion of these in exchange for goods made relatively land intensively abroad. This specialization has further consequences. As a result of it, labor at home becomes relatively more scarce, as does land abroad; therefore, the wage rate rises at home, as do land rents abroad. Under certain (very special) technical conditions, there will be a tendency toward the equalization of wage rates and land rents across both countries. This result is known as the "factor price equalization theorem." Samuelson derived a number of additional results from this simple model. One of them is the following: If there happens to be a rise in the price of a particular good, then this will eventually lead to an increase in the price of the factor that is used relatively intensively in the production of the good. This is known as the "Stolper-Samuelson theorem."

The reader will have noticed that the HOS model was originally formulated only as a model with two "original" or "primary" factors: land and labor. It was not formulated with reference to produced means of production or capital goods, and this for good reasons. The presence of capital goods causes difficulties that cast doubt on the widespread inclination of many economists to believe that the HOS results apply also to a world with heterogeneous capital goods. As the British economists Ian Steedman (b. 1941) and Stanley Metcalfe showed, several of the outcomes derived from the HOS framework do not generally hold in such a world. The so-called Leontief paradox points to the same issue. To his surprise, Wassily Leontief discovered in his much-debated 1953 contribution, "Domestic production and foreign trade: the American capital position re-examined," that the United States imports goods that are relatively capital intensive and exports ones that are relatively labor intensive, although the United States is considered a country with a relatively large capital endowment compared with the majority of its trading partners.

Several explanations of what is a "paradox" from the point of view of HOS theory have been put forward. It has been argued, among other things, that the HOS assumption that both countries are possessed of the same technical knowledge is untenable, because there is no costless transfer of technical knowledge from advanced countries to developing ones, nor are preferences of consumers the same. As a consequence of technological differences, the kinds of capital goods used and kinds of labor performed will partly be different. And when it comes to the heterogeneity of both capital and labor, what does it mean to say that one economy is better endowed in terms of capital than labor? Apparently the capital endowment can only be ascertained by rendering heterogeneous capital goods commensurable, which presupposes evaluating them in terms of their prices. There is simply no such thing as the "quantity of capital" in any economy that can be known prior to and independently of the prices of commodities—which in turn involves knowledge of income distribution. Also, to reckon an hour of skilled labor as equivalent to an hour of unskilled labor, as is typically done in many empirical studies, is inappropriate. In short, the HOS approach to international trade is difficult to sustain, and while it is still being taught and applied, it has lost much of its former reputation (see also chap. 12).

PUBLIC GOODS Samuelson also formulated a theory of public goods, elaborating on ideas formulated by Erik Lindahl. A public good differs from a private good in two respects: it is nonrival in consumption and it is also nonexcludable. While in the case of a private good, say a bar of chocolate, the good's consumption by one person prevents other persons from consuming it—it is rival in consumption. This is not so with regard to public goods, where one person's consumption does not compete with another person's consumption. A typical example given in the literature is that of the light from a lighthouse: it can warn the skippers of many ships about the danger of running onto the rocks. In the case of public goods it is also hardly possible to exclude anyone from consuming them: in the case of the lighthouse it would be very costly to prevent any one of the skippers seeing its light—public goods are nonexcludable.

Public goods, Samuelson insisted, raise the problem of "market failure": the producer of such a good bears all the costs but has difficulties collecting any revenue. "Free riders" use the good but do not make any contribution to defray its cost. These kinds of goods should therefore be provided by the public sector. In the case of a private good, the optimal amount to bring to the market is one for which consumers' marginal willingness to pay equals producers' marginal costs of production. In the case of a public good, Samuelson argued, the optimal quantity is the one at which the *sum* of the marginal propensities of all members of society to pay corresponds to the marginal (publicly funded) costs of production.

In spite of his decidedly neoclassical credo, Samuelson was also a Keynesian. His pathbreaking works on dynamic economic theory show that economic systems can react with sensitivity to changes in initial conditions and that there is no reason to assume they are always globally stable. (An equilibrium is said to be globally stable if the system approaches it irrespective of its starting point.) Samuelson saw the possibility of a cumulatively self-destabilizing economy described by Keynes not as an abstract case but a historically recurring fact that can only be dealt with using a policy of stabilization.

KENNETH J. ARROW Arrow, too, established new subfields (such as "health economics") and helped give a major impetus to already existing ones (such as "collective decision-making theory" and the "economics of information"). In *Social Choice and Individual Values* (1951), he tackled the relationship between the individual and society. How, Arrow asked, do we arrive at social decisions in democracies, and how do these relate to individual values?

Arrow's point of departure was the "Condorcet paradox," first introduced by the French mathematician and philosopher, the Marquis de Condorcet (1743–1794). Condorcet showed that, in a democratic process in which several policy options are subjected to paired majority decision making, the sequencing of votes can affect the outcome: a so-called Condorcet cycle. Assume that three persons are participating in a vote about three alternatives, X, Y, and Z. Person 1 favors X as the alternative to Y, and the latter in preference to Z, while Person 2 favors Y over Z and Z over X, with Person 3 preferring Z to X and X to Y. If the vote is framed as "X or Y," X will win by 2:1 votes, while Y is eliminated. If a vote about "X or Z" comes next, Z wins 2:1, and X is eliminated. Hence Z emerges as the victor, the decision has been made. The paradox is this: if Z were compared with Y, the already eliminated alternative Y would win by a vote of 2:1. With a different sequence of these paired votes, there would be a different outcome.

Investigating the Condorcet paradox for more general cases, Arrow arrived at his famous "impossibility theorem." He derived this for a set of abstract axioms or conditions (such as no restrictions on individual preferences, nondictatorship, etc.) that were considered plausible and did not require further justifications. The theorem says that for societies with three or more members, there is no procedure for deriving consistent social decisions from individual values. Social decisions, therefore, do not satisfy the same logic that underlies the theory of individual rational behavior—meaning that "society" cannot be treated as one representative individual. In general, there is no social welfare function, as the American economist Abram Bergson (1914–2003) and Paul Samuelson had posited in 1938 and 1947, respectively, that can be consistently derived from individual preferences and that could serve as a guiding principle for economic policy recommendations.

We may go one step further. If one takes into account that an individual acts in different social contexts and takes on different social roles (family, occupation, sports, politics, etc.) and one assumes that this individual has well-defined preferences peculiar to each context, then Arrow's impossibility theorem can even be applied to a single individual. It may explain why individuals experience cognitive dissonances and occasionally have difficulties making decisions, which may reflect conflicts between the different roles they perform. It may also explain the wisdom contained in David Hume's observation: "man is a heap of contradictions."

Arrow's impossibility theorem and the derivation of social decisions from individual preferences are still discussed to this day. The focus is on whether the axioms alluded to earlier are incontrovertible and what happens if some of them are weakened (discussed later).

Arrow, partly in cooperation with Gérard Debreu and Frank H. Hahn (1925–2013), also made major contributions to the "theory of general intertemporal equilibrium." Most notably, in their 1954 paper "Existence of an equilibrium for a competitive economy," Arrow and Debreu proved for the first time that an equilibrium exists, provided certain assumptions concerning agents' preferences and the set of technological alternatives are met. (The assumptions are fairly strong and are compatible with perfect competition, the workhorse of general equilibrium theory.) This result has been interpreted in very different ways. Hahn saw it as a kind of impossibility theorem: outside the realm to which the assumptions apply, there is no assurance of the existence of an equilibrium, and so the theory might be said to contribute little to deciphering reality, which does not obey the assumptions. Others contended that the model captures economic reality reasonably well. For example, so-called computable general equilibrium models, which consist of radically stripped-down versions of the Arrow-Debreu model, are widely used in applied economics, and Lucasian macroeconomics (dealt with in chap. 10) consist of a still more radically stripped-down version of it. Hahn was not convinced by these claims.

Up until now we have only been concerned with the problem of the existence of a general equilibrium. However, there are two other problems that must be briefly addressed. First, is the equilibrium unique, that is, is there only a single one, or are there several equilibria? If there are several equilibria, then the question is which of them is the relevant one, if any. This cannot be answered without having recourse to ad hoc assumptions that eliminate all equilibria except one—not a very comfortable situation. The second property is even more important than the one just discussed: Is the equilibrium stable, or is it unstable? As Alfred Marshall had already emphasized, the existence of an equilibrium is of little interest if the equilibrium is not also stable, meaning that deviations from it mobilize forces from within the economic system that lead back to it. In the latter case deviations would be self-correcting, whereas in the case of an unstable equilibrium deviations from it would be self-amplifying, and the concept of equilibrium as a point of rest, or attractor, would vanish.

The question of stability of a general equilibrium is intricate and for a long time could not be answered satisfactorily. Although many economists held strong beliefs about the stability of market systems, this was not supported by a compelling theoretical proof. Things changed only in the early 1970s with papers by Hugo F. Sonnenschein (b. 1940), Rolf Mantel (1934–1999), and Gérard Debreu. Alas, the results they came up with were rather sobering: things look bad for any proof of stability unless additional bold assumptions are piled upon the usual ones entertained in general equilibrium theory. The reason for this negative result is to be found in the interdependence of different markets: whatever happens on one market can be expected to affect what happens in all other markets and typically entails so-called income effects. Thus, lower wages on the labor market bring about a lower demand for consumer goods, which in turn causes less demand for labor, and so on. In a way, the circular-flow relationships characterizing an economy, which Keynes had emphasized, spoil the dish. In view of the negative result regarding stability Martin Hellwig (b. 1949) spoke of the general equilibrium theory of the Arrow-Debreu variety as a "failed research program."

Arrow has since expressed a certain disenchantment with the theory for which he was awarded the Swedish Riksbank Prize in Economic Sciences.

He pointed to the difficulty, if not the impossibility, of predicting future economic events, given that economic agents base their decisions on their expectations of the behavior of others, which in turn is based on the expected behavior of yet others and so on. This necessitates, as Keynes had stressed especially with regard to financial markets, forming expectations about other people's expectations. The economist, who seeks to predict the development of an economy, is thus faced with the Herculean task of predicting all these interrelated expectations.

Arrow insisted that a market system, to be perfect, would need markets for all products and services to exist from now to infinity. However, there is no complete set of markets and in fact there cannot be such a complete set at any moment of time. Think, for example, of products that have not yet been invented or generally of innovations—Schumpeter's grand theme. This is why Arrow distanced himself from a fundamental assumption underlying general equilibrium theory—an assumption that was also forcefully advocated by Hayek and his followers—namely that prices contain all the information needed to make decisions. Against this Arrow emphasized that a great deal of important information is not conveyed by the price system. This is exemplified by prices at the stock market immediately before a bubble bursts. These prices say very little about the true worth of assets. From these considerations it follows that the "efficient market hypothesis" with regard to financial markets is difficult to sustain (see chap. 12).

These considerations already anticipated Arrow's pioneering work in the economics of information, which deals with the role of uncertainty, incomplete and asymmetrical information, and moral hazard. He modeled the kind of risk aversion that shows up in the purchase of risky securities and insurance policies as an expression of weighing higher risk against a higher expected value for real income. Arrow also integrated the problems of uncertainty and risk into the general intertemporal equilibrium model, providing the basis for modern capital market theory and for an analysis of financial markets—how they function and how they fail. The problem of asymmetrical information and of moral hazard, another focus of Arrow, has had implications for topics as diverse as the patient-physician relationship and buying used cars. Arrow argued that relationships of trust that can develop between agents may be seen as a substitute for ideal insurance markets, which do not exist.

AMARTYA SEN In *Collective Choice and Social Welfare* (1971), the Indian-born Harvard economist Amartya Sen (b. 1933) tackled Arrow's impossibility theorem by changing its axioms—leading to "possibility theorems." He discussed, for example, the implication of granting each person the right to veto a policy or social choice on the basis of his or her own preferences. In addition, he developed a further impossibility theorem—that of the "impossibility of a Paretian liberal." This refers to the clash between the conditions for Pareto optimality and the minimal requirements for individual liberty when any kind of preferences are allowed. Sen provided the following example: a prude would not enjoy reading an allegedly pornographic book (*Lady Chatterley's Lover*), but would like even less for a letch to read the book and take delight in it. The letch, by contrast, would gladly read the book but would prefer even more to have the prude read the book and suffer from that reading. Can one demand, in the name of freedom, that neither one reads the book, even though the letch would like to read it? No. Can one demand, in the name of freedom, that the prude must read the book even though he or she does not want to? No. The only remaining alternative is for the letch to read it. But, according to their preferences, what has priority for both persons is that the prude reads the book and the letch does not.

Proceeding from the *A Theory of Justice* by John Rawls (1921–2002), published in 1971, and the theory of collective decisions, Sen also constructed indexes to measure income and welfare inequality and in 1976 proposed a new poverty index. He was intensely concerned with the problem of famines and argued that these are less drastic in democratic societies because the poor have a voice. Poverty is not so much a question of income, Sen insisted, as of the rights, liberties, and capabilities that people have and that require support.

Sen calls the *homo economicus* who only maximizes his self-interest a "rational fool" in his essay "Rational fools: a critique of the behavioral foundations of economic theory" (1977) and offers the following example: A asks B the way to the railway station. The latter shows him the way to the post office and asks him, if he should accidentally pass by a post office, to drop off a letter for him there. A agrees, having resolved to open the letter at the next opportunity to see if it contains anything valuable. The message Sen wishes to convey by means of this example is that if the world were populated by people who only care about themselves, as is assumed in much of economic theory, the game of human society will go on miserably. In short, the *homo economicus*, while useful in some limited contexts, does not provide an adequate starting point for a social theory eager to explain reality.

In the concluding chapter we discuss a few selected fields in which important developments have taken place since the middle of the twentieth century. (Other such fields, for example, evolutionary economics, have already been touched upon earlier.) Though the developments are new, most of these fields reach far back into the history of economics. Once again it has to be stressed that this is not a comprehensive account, let alone complete. Its main aim is to illustrate the fact that the subject of economics is alive and thriving and that new developments are often firmly rooted in the ideas and concepts formulated a long time ago.

12

DEVELOPMENTS IN
SELECTED FIELDS

GAME THEORY Contrary to the assumption of perfect competition, according to which no economic agent has any market power and all are fully informed about all economically relevant matters, many firms in the real world do have market power and are not fully informed about the competitors they interact with in the market: if a firm undertakes certain actions, it has to reckon with reactions from competitors, and vice versa. Strategic interaction takes the place of adjustment to given circumstances. This kind of behavior is what game theory investigates. It uses sophisticated mathematical tools to deal with problems not only in economics, but also in many other fields, especially in politics and in military and social conflicts.

The roots of game theory go back several centuries, to the Swiss mathematician Daniel Bernoulli (1700–1782). Bernoulli worked at the czar's court in St. Petersburg and posed the question of how to put a monetary value on the following game: a coin is tossed for as long as it takes for "tails" to appear. So long as "heads" appears, the player receives two ducats in the first round, four ducats in the second, eight in the third, and so on, doubling from one round to the next.

What, Bernoulli asked, is the "expected value of the game"—the probabilistic gain that one can expect before the game begins? The probability is 1/2 that "tails" will appear in the first round, 1/4 that it will appear in the second round, 1/8 in the third round, and so forth. The expected value is the sum of the payoffs weighted by their respective probabilities: $(1/2)2 + (1/4)4 + (1/8)8 + \ldots = 1 + 1 + 1 + \ldots$ to infinity. The resulting sum is infinitely large because the game can theoretically go on infinitely so long as "tails" does not appear. Theoretically, therefore, the player should be willing to pay a huge sum to take part in the game. But this contradicts actual life experience; nobody would pay an exorbitant sum to participate.

How did Bernoulli solve this paradox? In his view, we assess the game not according to the anticipated monetary gain but according to the expected utility. The utility for the player, he argued, does indeed rise with the gain, but less than proportionally: the increment of added utility provided by each additional expected unit of money sinks and approaches nil. (This assumption we have already encountered in chap. 4 when dealing with marginal utility theory.)

The "expected utility theorem" that underpins Bernoulli's hypothesis was used by the two founders of modern game theory to derive axioms for describing rational behavior: the Hungarian mathematician and natural scientist Janos (later John) von Neumann, who started out in 1928 analyzing whether there was a mathematical structure behind parlor games like chess or poker, and the Austrian economist Oskar Morgenstern. It was only after Morgenstern joined von Neumann at Princeton that the latter turned to the analysis of economic problems. Their *Theory of Games and Economic Behavior* (1944) is regarded as the cradle of modern game theory.

While much of conventional economic theory presupposes agents that are independent of one another, game theoretical models focus attention on interacting agents. In such "games" agents may enter binding agreements among themselves. In this case we speak of "cooperative games." If they do not, we speak of "noncooperative games."

The book by von Neumann and Morgenstern triggered a number of developments in the subject, whose growing importance in the last century is indicated by the many game theorists who were awarded the Swedish Riksbank Prize in Economic Sciences.

A simple game is the two-person zero-sum game, in which the sum of the payoffs of the two players is zero irrespective of the game's final outcome, because whatever one player gains, the other one loses. (Poker is an example of a zero-sum game.) A solution to this two-person game was already provided in von Neumann's (German) 1928 paper and then also in his book with Morgenstern. Generalizing this to n ($n > 2$) persons (with variable sums) proved to be difficult and was solved only by John Forbes Nash in two papers published in 1950, one devoted to noncooperative (competitive) games, the other to cooperative games. The competitive solution of n-person variable sum games, as we have already learned, is known as the "Nash equilibrium." It corresponds to a set of strategies, one for each agent, that provide no incentive to any of the agents for unilaterally changing his or her strategy. Nash's respective result is now widely used in microeconomic textbooks. Nash studied the cooperative solution for two-person variable sum games that satisfy a number of suitable axioms. In a paper published in 1953 he investigated another type of cooperative solution, which he called a "threatening solution," when cooperation among agents is effectuated by coercion.

In the 1950s, the so-called prisoner's dilemma achieved special fame. Here is a simple description of what it is all about: Two prison inmates who are both accused of having committed a crime together are interrogated separately. If neither confesses, they will receive a relatively mild sentence (four years, say). If both confess, both receive a harsher sentence (seven years). However, if one confesses (thus implicating them both) and the other does not, the one who has confessed receives a shorter sentence (three years) than if both had confessed, although the one who denies guilt will get a higher sentence than in all the other cases (twelve years).

Independent of what the other does, confession is the best option—the "dominant strategy"—for both, which earns them seven years in prison. The resulting noncooperative equilibrium may be individually rational in that it minimizes the maximum penalty for both (7, 7), but it is not the collectively rational option, for mutual denial would mean only four years in prison for each. This would be the cooperative equilibrium, the solution the two would reach with a binding agreement, which, however, is improbable in the situation under consideration. Expressed in more general terms, individually rational behavior can lead to collectively less favorable results than can cooperation.

Game theory has broad applicability and is very much a child of the "East-West conflict" that intensified as a result of the rise of the Soviet Union in the mid-twentieth century. Von Neumann was involved in the Manhattan Project and in building both the A-bomb and the H-bomb.

As tensions with the Soviet Union grew, von Neumann was appointed to the position of a strategic adviser on defense policy. Game theory was employed in developing the doctrine of "mutually assured destruction" that shaped U.S. strategy during the Cold War.

CAPITAL THEORY In the 1960s and 1970s, a controversy over capital theory erupted between the adherents of classical and Keynesian approaches, on the one hand, and neoclassical approaches, on the other. Since the chief players in this debate came from Cambridge in the United Kingdom (Joan Robinson, Piero Sraffa, Nicholas Kaldor, Luigi Pasinetti, and Pierangelo Garegnani) and Cambridge in Massachusetts (Paul A. Samuelson and Robert Solow), this has also been known as the "Cambridge controversies." While at first sight the controversies might appear to have concerned arcane technical matters, they in fact concerned the tenability, or otherwise, of the two main pillars upon which mainstream economics rests: Say's law, according to which the market economy tends to utilize all productive resources at its disposal (full employment); and marginal productivity theory, according to which the resulting product is shared out among the various claimants according to their marginal contributions to the product. The Cambridge (UK) critics disputed the validity of the two closely intertwined propositions.

The controversy started with an essay by Robinson (1953) in which she rejected the neoclassical macroeconomic production function $Y = f(K, L)$, with Y representing national product, K capital stock, and L labor input, as untenable because it did not adequately describe an economy using and producing heterogeneous goods. In 1962, Samuelson replied with an essay meant to show that the concept is capable of adequately depicting microeconomic conditions. To this effect he used a model in which two goods are produced: a pure consumption good and a capital good that is used as an input both in the production of itself and in the production of the consumption good. He allowed for many techniques of production for the two goods that could be chosen by cost-minimizing producers. He showed that the model exhibits properties that mimic those of the (in)famous macroeconomic production function. In particular, he argued that in competitive conditions the marginal productivities of labor and capital were equal to the real wage rate and the rate of profits, respectively. In this way, he felt, he had demonstrated that the economic system as a whole can be analyzed in terms of the macroeconomic production function.

The subsequent debate showed that this was not true in general. In a paper published in 1970 Pierangelo Garegnani proved that Samuelson's argument was only valid if all sectors of the economy—in Samuelson's case the sector producing the capital good and the sector producing the consumption good—have under all circumstances the same input ratio of capital to labor (or capital intensity). However, if this is the case, the sectors cannot be distinguished from one another in terms of their use of inputs, and it is somewhat mysterious how the same set of inputs could result in qualitatively different outputs. As Garegnani stressed, Samuelson's assumption of equal input proportions across all sectors effectively amounts to assuming a world with a single good only. Outside such a world marginal productivity theory does not generally hold, and therefore income distribution cannot generally be explained in terms of it.

In the course of the debate it emerged that Sraffa (1960), with his revival of classical analysis (see chap. 3), had also provided the foundation for a critique of marginalist theory.

The critique essentially revolves around two propositions by Sraffa. First, the capital used in production by a firm, a sector, or the entire economy consists of different kinds of capital goods. In order to indicate the "quantity of capital" employed relative to labor, individual capital goods have to be valued and then added up at their respective prices. But as we previously saw in the discussion of production prices (chap. 2), prices depend not only on the technology used but also on income distribution, that is, the level of the real wage rate. With the real wage rate fixed at a different level and with the possible differences in the techniques chosen by cost-minimizing producers, the corresponding rate of profits and relative prices will generally be different. Now the "quantity of capital," being a value sum, cannot be ascertained prior to knowing the prices of commodities and thus independently of the real wage rate: it can only be determined simultaneously with prices and the rate of profits. But marginal productivity theory attempts to determine the general rate of profits as an expression of the relative scarcity of a given quantity of capital. Since this already presupposes knowledge of the profit rate, we are confronted with a circular argument.

Sraffa's second proposition was that, contrary to the widely held neoclassical view, a higher real wage rate (which corresponds to a lower rate of profits) does not necessarily lead to choosing a production technique in a single firm, an industry, or even the economy as a whole that uses relatively less labor and more capital (in other words, a technique that exhibits a higher capital intensity or capital-to-labor ratio). At first sight the idea that whatever becomes more expensive (in the case discussed here: labor) will be substituted for is highly plausible. But since capital is a value magnitude, it is possible that prices change in such a way (consequent upon an increase in the real wage rate) that the ratio of capital to labor used in a sector or in the economy as a whole does not increase, but decreases. This possibility is known as "capital reversing." Sraffa also showed that the technical alternatives available to firms cannot generally be ordered with the level of the rate of profits in such a way that the lower the rate of profits, the larger the capital intensity: it is possible that the same technique is cost minimizing both at low and high levels of the rate of profits, with one or several other techniques being cost minimizing at intermediate levels of the rate of profits. This possibility is known as "reswitching of a technique." For a summary account of the debates in capital theory, see Harcourt (1972).

These seemingly abstract findings have, according to the critics of economic orthodoxy, an eminently practical meaning in that they run counter to Say's law. They undermine the common notion that unemployment is *always* attributable to wages that are "too high" and can only be eliminated by cutting wages.

Sraffa's reformulation of the classical approach was further developed by, among others, Garegnani, Luigi Pasinetti (b. 1930), Neri Salvadori (b. 1951), Bertram Schefold (b. 1943), Ian Steedman, and Christian Bidard (b. 1948). In *Full Industry Equilibrium*, published in 2015, Arrigo Opocher (b. 1954) and Ian Steedman show that the conventional long-run theory of input demand and output supply taught in microeconomics cannot be sustained, as it is based on the assumption that just *one* price can be changed at a time. Yet this is not possible: at least some other price must change as a consequence of the first change. But once this is taken into account, it becomes clear that the quantity of an input employed need not always be inversely related to its price. In other words, the usually assumed demand curve of an input (labor, raw materials, etc.) that is negatively elastic with regard to the input's price cannot generally be sustained.

GROWTH THEORY Ever since the inception of systematic economic analysis at the time of the classical authors, growth and development have been among the central topics of economics. However, in terms of substance things have changed considerably over time. While in Adam Smith's work economic growth and development were seen to be intimately intertwined and a result of the endogenous forces at work within the economy, at the beginning of the twentieth century a new perspective on the problem gradually gained importance. It focused on (quantitative) growth, setting aside (qualitative and structural) development, and saw growth essentially as reflecting exogenous forces. The upshot of this change was Robert Solow's neoclassical growth model published (in a 1956 paper) as a reaction especially to Harrod's work in the area. (In the same year the Australian economist Trevor Swan [1918–1989] published a similar model.)

The difference between the Smithian approach to the problem and Solow's can be illustrated in terms of how they dealt with the main factors affecting growth and development: (1) technical and organizational change, (2) capital accumulation, and (3) growth of population and employment. While Smith discussed technical and organizational change in terms of an ever-deeper division of social labor and saw it thus both as the result and the driving force of economic development, Solow took the rate of technical progress as given from outside the system—he treated it as an *exogenous* variable: technical progress falls like "manna from heaven." While for Smith the accumulation of capital, by expanding the extent of markets, fosters the ongoing process of the division of labor and brings about new goods, new means of production, and structural change (from agriculture to manufacturing, commerce, and foreign trade), in Solow's macroeconomic approach more "capital" simply means more of the same stuff. While in Smith the growth of population is determined endogenously, reflecting economic, social, and institutional factors at work, in Solow the rate of growth of population is given from the outside and is thus also treated as an exogenous variable.

The aim of Solow's model was to discuss the case in which there are ample opportunities for substitution between the only two factors of production considered, homogeneous labor and homogeneous capital— contrary to Harrod, who had assumed a relatively rigid input proportion. Solow described technical alternatives in terms of a particular version of the macroeconomic production function—the so-called Cobb-Douglas function, $Y = AK^{\alpha} L^{1-\alpha}$ named after the American economists Charles Cobb (1875–1949) and Paul Douglas (1892–1976), where A and α are given (positive) parameters. (It deserves to be mentioned that the works of Knut Wicksell and the English economist Philip Wicksteed [1844–1927] toward the end of the nineteenth century had already discussed this function.) Land was subsumed under the factor "capital" and therefore no longer played any independent role in the argument. Cobb and Douglas adopted this form not to express any production theoretic relationship but to mimic a stylized fact of the time: the relative constancy of the share of profits and the share of wages in national income, the former being given by the parameter α, the latter by $1 - \alpha$. If interpreted as a production function, as in Solow, the Cobb-Douglas function exhibits constant returns to scale and positive but diminishing marginal productivities with respect to the two factors, capital and labor.

Solow assumed that the economy is at any moment in a dynamic equilibrium, meaning that all markets are simultaneously cleared, labor is thus fully employed, and the capital stock fully utilized. As Solow emphasized, it is a "straight rope view" of economic growth. He justified it on the ground that Keynesian aggregate-demand management successfully stabilized the economy. Given these premises, how would the economy grow over time? Since all factors of production are always fully used, the growth of the gross national product (GNP) is decided by the growth of the two factors, labor and capital, contributing to its production. The labor force was assumed to grow at an exogenously given and constant rate, the "natural rate of growth," λ, while the growth of the capital stock was governed by the savings behavior of agents. In accordance with Say's law, Solow assumed that all savings would be invested (that is, there is no separate investment function in his model). He developed his argument in terms of a simple proportional savings function, which in obvious notation can be written as: $S = sY = I = \Delta K$. Hence both the labor force and the capital stock will grow over time and with them the social product.

If the capital stock happens to grow more (or less) swiftly than the labor force, capital will become relatively less (or more) scarce than labor, and its marginal productivity will fall (or rise), whereas the marginal productivity of labor will rise (or fall). This, however, has a weakening (or strengthening) effect on capital accumulation. As a consequence, the growth rate of the capital stock and that of the social product will converge over time toward the exogenously given rate of growth of the workforce. In what is called the "steady state," all rates will be equal to one another and equal to the natural rate of growth, λ. Hence it would not be misleading to say that in the long run, growth in the Solow model is not explained but given from the outside.

Solow's model and his own empirical testing of it gave rise to a huge business called "growth accounting." On the basis of time series for capital stock and employment and observed factor shares (share of profits and share of wages), Solow used his model to predict what the growth rate of GNP should have been in the period under consideration on the assumption that his model was correct. He then compared this hypothetical rate with the actual one and found to his great surprise that the former significantly underestimated the latter. Depending on the country and the period under consideration, the "unexplained rest" ranged from around 30 to 60 percent. The American economist Moses Abramovitz (1912–2000) called this rest "a measure of our ignorance." Solow swiftly attributed the failure of his model to the fact that an important force of growth had been left out of consideration: technological progress. He attributed the entire unexplained rest to the working of this force and thus implicitly contended that there was nothing wrong with the macroeconomic production function. He treated technical progress as an exogenously given factor that exerts its influence as time goes by and replaced the production function $Y = f(K, L)$ by $Y = F(K, L, t)$, where t represents time, which is seen as the vehicle that brings a steady increase in technical knowledge. With the rate of increase of the latter given, the natural rate of growth consists now of two components: the given rate of growth of labor plus the also given rate of growth of labor productivity.

Solow's model is still very popular in macroeconomics and empirical research. However, soon after its publication it was already subjected to a number of criticisms. We have already encountered the objections leveled at the concept of the macroeconomic production function and the concept of capital entertained in it. Other objections concerned the predictions implicit in the model. Think of two economies, one developed, the other not, possessed of the same technical knowledge, the same propensity to save, and the same natural rate of growth, but with the former employing a larger amount of capital per worker than the latter. According to Solow, the latter economy would grow more swiftly than the former and would gradually "catch up" with it. The model thus predicts a convergence in the per capita incomes of the two countries. Alas, this was not generally confirmed by the facts. While some less-developed economies managed to catch up with industrialized economies and a few even to surpass them (think of the so-called Asian tigers), others fell behind (think of sub-Saharan countries in Africa). Apparently, while the factors contemplated by the Solow model (capital, labor, and technology) play an important role in the process of economic development and growth, they are by no means the only ones and, what is more, Solow's conceptualization of them and their interplay is perhaps difficult to sustain.

It was not only the Cambridge (UK) critics of neoclassicism who entertained this view but also, albeit for different reasons, the representatives of what became known as "new" or "endogenous" growth theory, which started to flourish in the second half of the 1980s. Two closely connected aspects of Solow's model in particular were found wanting. First, the model lacked a microeconomic explanation of why the behavior of agents led to growth in income per capita. Second, technical progress must not be taken as given but interpreted as the outcome of the self-interested decisions taken by individuals. Otherwise contributions to new growth theory basically accepted the Solovian macroeconomic (one-good), full employment framework and focused attention on the formalization of a number of endogenous mechanisms propelling the system forward.

In a paper published in 1986 ("Increasing returns and long-run growth"), the American economist Paul Romer (b. 1955) contemplated the role of firms in generating new, economically useful knowledge. He argued that firms produce not only goods but also, in their R&D departments, new knowledge. By means of this they intend to improve their position vis-à-vis their rivals in the competitive struggle. The important point in Romer's argument is that the new knowledge they generate is a quasi-public good. This means that it is nonrival in consumption—the use of a new industrial device such as the Bessemer process in steel production by one firm does not preclude its use also by other firms—and other potential users can only temporarily be excluded access to it. In short, sooner or later the new knowledge becomes generally available. While initially an invention increases only the productivity of the firm that has developed it, the public good character of knowledge eventually increases the productivity of other firms in the market. At this point we are again confronted with the problem of market failure that is notorious when it comes to public goods: The innovating firm bears the cost of the invention in terms of its R&D expenditures, but it does not receive all the resultant benefits (profits). This acts as a brake upon inventive activities, reflected in too little R&D. As in other cases of public goods, the government is called upon to raise R&D from suboptimal levels.

From a sociology of science point of view, it is interesting to note that this argument was forged in view of the remarkable success of Japanese companies, especially car manufacturers, on the world market. Inquiring into the causes of this success, the Japanese Ministry of International Trade and Industry (MITI) came to the fore. MITI effectively shaped Japanese industrial policy, funded and coordinated research among firms and universities, and directed investment. The title of the book *The Entrepreneurial State* (2013) by Mariana Mazzucato (b. 1968) expresses well the role of the government in this regard. The book illustrates in terms of multiple examples (especially from Silicon Valley) that high-risk investments by the state may be a prerequisite for business investments. The widespread view of an inefficient state hampering the activities of an efficient private sector has thus to be relegated at least partly to the realm of fiction.

In a paper published in 1988 ("On the mechanics of economic development"), Robert Lucas put forward a parallel argument to the one furnished by Romer. He focused attention on the formation of human capital and its individual and collective effects. People wish to improve their skills and capabilities in the hope and expectation that this will give them access to better-paying and more interesting jobs. But by communicating and cooperating with others, their knowledge will be shared and increase human capital. Again we are confronted with a spillover effect or a positive externality of self-interested behavior. And again there is a public good problem, because the single agent yields only a part of the benefits generated by his or her investment in human capital formation.

Parallel to new growth theory, Keynesian and Kaleckian approaches were developed in which the principle of effective demand was extended to the long run. According to these approaches there is no presumption that the economy will gravitate around a path characterized by the full employment of labor and full capacity utilization, as in the models dealt with up until now, in which it is assumed that Say's law holds true. The economic system is seen to be demand constrained most of the time and supply constrained only in rare and fairly short intervals of time.

Highly developed economies with a large stock of durable capital goods (plant and equipment) are characterized by a high "elasticity of production": by way of an adjustable capacity utilization rate, they can flexibly react to fluctuating levels of effective demand. The point of departure is the Keynesian "paradox of thrift": if there is an autonomous rise in savings but no parallel rise in investments, this leads via a decrease in effective demand to a recession. In this case, an austerity policy is a recessionary policy. If, on the other hand, there is an autonomous rise in investments, then this will engender in the short run an increase in effective demand, capacity utilization, employment, national income, and savings. In the medium and long run a brisk effective demand may induce further investments (the accelerator effect), which in turn entail further savings and thus a higher pace of capital accumulation and economic growth. Depending on the exact shape of the investment and savings function, one obtains different "regimes": while in "profit-led regimes" lower wages stimulate investment activity and growth via rising profits, in "wage-led regimes" higher wages cause higher growth by way of the rising demand for consumer goods. There is, accordingly, no passe-partout economic policy, no one-size-fits-all approach that has the desired effect everywhere and always.

The models elaborated also discuss the relationship between effective demand, market structure, and technical progress on the one hand and the interaction between the monetary and financial sphere of the economy and its real sphere on the other. The focus has recently shifted to the "financialization" of contemporary capitalism; that is, the dramatic rise in the importance of the financial sector relative to industry and other producing sectors. As we have seen, this development was foreshadowed in Rudolf Hilferding's *Finance Capital* (1910).

Important contributions to this literature came from, among others, the Austrian Josef Steindl (1912–1993), the Indian Amit Bhaduri (b. 1940), and the American Stephen Marglin (b. 1938).

SPATIAL AND URBAN ECONOMICS Large parts of economic theory implicitly assume that neglecting the fact that all economic activity has a spatial dimension—production, work, consumption, and so on must take place somewhere—has no appreciable influence on the results obtained. (According to the physicist John Wheeler [1911–2008], "space is what prevents everything from happening to me," while "time is what prevents everything from happening at once.") This view cannot be sustained. Since economic agents cannot but occupy different positions in space, some more favorable than others, perfect competition cannot prevail. David Starrett (b. 1942) demonstrated in his 1978 paper "Market allocations of location choice in a model with free mobility" what was called his "spatial impossibility theorem," that is, the competitive price mechanism formalized by Arrow and Debreu can explain neither the emergence of spatial economic concentration nor extensive trade streams. With constant returns to scale economic activity will be evenly distributed across a homogeneous plain, carried out by autarkic units of production and consumption.

According to Paul Samuelson, Johann Heinrich von Thünen was "the founding god" of spatial economics. As early as 1826, in his book *The Isolated State*, he developed a theory of the spatial distribution of primary production (agriculture and forestry) on a plain surrounding a town that serves as the marketplace. There is a clear division of labor between town and country. In the town, manufactures are produced and services offered in exchange for agricultural products coming from the country. Around the town arise concentric circles, Thünen's famous rings, in which—depending on transportation costs, the perishability of products, the intensity of cultivation, and so on—a specific configuration of activities takes hold as the distance from the city increases and population density decreases. These rings result from the cost-minimizing behavior of producers.

Thünen's model did a good job of interpreting settlement and production patterns in preindustrial societies such as, for example, in Tuscany, Italy. However, his work extends far beyond the ring model and investigates, among others, the choice of location of towns and invokes cumulative causation mechanisms as Adam Smith had mentioned in his analysis of the social division of labor (and as will be discussed in more detail here). Since several of Thünen's manuscripts have not yet been published, many of his innovative findings have yet to see the light of the day.

Partly in the footsteps of Thünen, German economists made major contributions to the study of the location problem and the spatial division of labor. Alfred Weber (1868–1958) identified "agglomeration effects" as an important factor in the location decision of firms in his *Theory of the Location of Industries* (1909). By this he meant both positive and negative external effects resulting from the concentration of firms in confined areas. The positive externalities include, for example, improved information exchange between firms and reduced transport and communication costs, whereas the negative ones include rising land prices, traffic jams, and pollution. W. Brian Arthur (b. 1946) built on such ideas to show that, owing to positive agglomeration effects, development is path dependent (as explored in his 1994 collection, *Increasing Returns and Path Dependence in the Economy*). The first firm to settle in the area bases its location decision solely on geographical preference. The second firm also takes into account the expected agglomeration benefit it will get if it settles in the vicinity of the first. Silicon Valley could have emerged somewhere else, but historical contingencies and self-reinforcing effects have made it what it is today. A region can get "locked in"—that is, it can take a path that is attractive in the short run but inferior in the long run. It may gradually lose its competitive edge because of negative externalities that begin to overwhelm the positive ones as the agglomeration process proceeds. But now sunk costs are high and capital cannot easily be withdrawn and invested elsewhere. This is the curse, for example, of old industrial regions that once were prosperous but then declined.

Walter Christaller (1893–1969) and August Lösch (1906–1945) elaborated early mathematical analyses of the spatial order of the economy in books published in 1933 and 1940, respectively. Christaller showed that settlements in a region typically exhibit a spatial-functional relationship to one another and·represent different levels of a hierarchical structure: the larger the number of key goods and services supplied in a settlement (city, town, village) the more central it is. Under certain assumptions, market areas corresponding to settlements take a hexagonal form (as in a beehive). Historians have used this approach to explain settlement structures in the late Middle Ages and the early modern era. The American Walter Isard (1919–2010), with his 1956 book *Location and Space-Economy*, is widely considered the "father of regional science." It always helps to stand on the shoulders of giants.

In the urban economics of William Alonso (1933–1999), the central business district (CBD), as described in his 1964 book *Location and Land Use*, takes the place of Thünen's market square. "Clustering" of firms happens because of positive externalities. What characterizes a monocentric city is that land rent, land prices, and population density decrease with growing distance from the city center. Faster and less expensive means of transportation explain the evening out of urban population density, leading to suburbanization and urban sprawl. But the clustering of firms also has negative external effects, as analyzed already by Weber, and leads to longer commutes from home to work. Negative externalities can ultimately lead to multiple CBDs within a single city.

Another topic of urban economics is "segregation"—for example, the racial division of residential districts. One explanation for this is racism; the observed macrophenomenon is an expression of micromotivations. Thomas Schelling (b. 1921) presented a different view in his classic work *Micromotives and Macrobehavior* (1978). Segregation, Schelling showed, could occur even without racial dispositions, as the following example illustrates: on a chessboard, some green and some red figures are placed arbitrarily, but with several squares left free. Each figure now prefers a square where, among eight potential neighboring squares, not more than four are occupied by figures of the other color. If this condition is met, the well-being of the figure equals 1, otherwise it is equal to 0. Now, little by little, each other figure is given the chance to move to a preferred square. If its well-being in the initial situation is equal to 0, then it can switch to a neighboring free square where its well-being is positive. In the case of a well-being of 1, there are no grounds for changing places. After just a few rounds, the trend to segregation in enclosed red and green spaces becomes apparent.

DEVELOPMENT ECONOMICS AND THE NEW ECONOMIC GEOGRAPHY Adam Smith had emphasized that the international division of labor brings about gains of specialization that in turn may lead to a further deepening of the division of labor. A virtuous circle makes successful firms and nations even more successful. In a 1957 book, Gunnar Myrdal (1898–1987) developed this further with his principle of "circular and cumulative causation." The Smithian case of a virtuous circle can be summarized as follows: capital accumulation increases the extent of markets, which allows the deepening of the division of labor, which increases productivity and incomes, especially profits, which leads to further capital accumulation, and so on. But circular and cumulative causation may also work in the opposite direction. As Myrdal showed, poor nations may be subject to a "vicious circle" and can become even poorer in the course of time. The important point to note here is that dynamic processes may amplify a positive or negative trend; there is no equilibrium. There is now a huge literature on so-called poverty traps, explaining why some less-developed countries find it so difficult to get out of misery.

New "economic geography" revolves essentially around the principle of circular and cumulative causation. The American economist Paul Krugman (b. 1953) showed in his 1991 paper "Increasing returns and economic geography" that on the basis of the principle, it is possible to explain a division of the "world" into core and periphery. If transportation costs are relatively low, then all (spatially) footloose industries, which are characterized by increasing returns to scale, will concentrate in a central region (the "north"), while the peripheral region (the "south") will produce standardized or homogeneous products (simple foodstuffs and raw materials). This economic polarization, or core-periphery structure, is an unintended consequence of self-interested behavior.

The process of deindustrialization that takes place in a number of industrialized economies can be attributed to several factors, including the following one. According to the product life-cycle theory developed by Raymond Vernon (1919–1999) in his paper "International investment and international trade in the product cycle" published in 1966, as a rule a product is first produced in the country in which it was invented and at the time typically represents a high-tech product. When the product is used throughout the world, production gradually moves away from the point of origin to less-developed countries, because with technical progress and the change in prices and wages it entails comparative advantage will change as well, and as a consequence so does the international division of labor. Think of the relocation of car manufacturing within and between nations.

PUBLIC CHOICE Many models that consider the behavior of the public sector assume implicitly that public servants act exclusively in the general interest. But as Adam Smith had already emphasized, there are no grounds to make such a bold assumption. Public servants can safely be assumed to act also in their own interest. This is the insight from which James Buchanan (1919–2013) and Gordon Tullock (1922–2014) developed "public choice theory." They mistrusted conventional welfare theory because it conveyed a totally unrealistic picture of public decision makers. Rather, they argued, it is necessary to draft laws and institutions that establish incentives so that politicians and bureaucrats in pursuit of their own interests simultaneously promote the public interest. In particular, rules need to be installed that make it difficult for politicians to increase the tax burden. As Schumpeter is reputed to have said: expecting a politician to exercise budgetary restraint is just as naïve as expecting a hound not to touch a sausage collection he has sniffed out.

BEHAVIORAL ECONOMICS AND EXPERIMENTAL ECONOMICS

Dissatisfied with the limited explanatory potential of models that take *homo economicus* as their point of departure, some scholars, irrespective of whether they were conscious of it or not, returned to the wealth of insights found in the behavioral theory of Hume and Smith. However, the research methods used were largely new and contradicted a long-standing opinion that economics could not use controlled experiments. In the most often cited paper ever, published in *Econometrica* in 1979, the Israeli-American cognitive psychologists Daniel Kahneman (b. 1934) and Amos Tversky (1937–1996) documented a number of behaviors that would be judged as anomalies and irrationalities in terms of the conventional theory of rational behavior. They focused on people's behavior under risk and uncertainty, which explains the title they gave their studies: prospect theory. People typically do not know the probabilities of outcomes and therefore cannot base their decisions on them. They base them instead on the expected potential value of gains and losses. Among Kahneman and Tversky's findings are the following. Whether people behave in a risk-averse or a risk-seeking manner depends on the way in which a choice is put to them. Hence there is what is called a "framing effect." They also found that people's attitudes toward risks concerning gains is often very different from their attitudes toward risks concerning losses. In fact, in many experiments people strongly preferred avoiding a loss of a certain magnitude over acquiring a gain of the same magnitude. This is also known as the "endowment effect": people attribute a higher value to a good they possess than to an identical good they do not possess. Loss aversion appears to be an important human attitude and must not be brushed aside as "irrational."

These results violate the axioms of expected utility theory put forward by von Neumann and Morgenstern, who stipulated that decisions are taken on the basis of known probabilities of outcomes. The results also contradict the Coase theorem, which implies there are no framing effects. Kahneman and Tversky advocated abandoning received utility theory and replacing it with an approach that is more solidly founded on the actual behavior of people and not on that of a fictional character.

Their paper triggered an avalanche of contributions and experimental studies that provided further empirical evidence of what look like anomalies and contradictions, if assessed in terms of received utility theory. There has also been recent research into what happens in the brain while humans make decisions. This has bolstered findings like that of loss aversion. In the context of recent experimental capital market research, such as the one conducted by Vernon Smith (b. 1927), insights from behavioral economics have contributed to explaining infectious and herd behavior. Much of the work of behavioral economists refutes the "efficient markets hypothesis" advocated by Chicago economists. Other important contributions to behavioral economics came, among others, from the Austrian Ernst Fehr (b. 1956).

Let me finally mention briefly two further areas in which a lot of research has been carried out in recent years.

NEW INSTITUTIONAL ECONOMICS The so-called new institutional economics (as opposed to old institutional economics touched upon in chap. 7) goes back to the British economist Ronald Coase. He inquired into reasons for the existence of hierarchical organizations, such as firms (1937). Why, he asked, aren't all economic transactions carried out via markets? The reason, he stressed, is transaction costs, like search and information costs, that occur when markets are used but that can be reduced by establishing firms. Oliver Williamson (b. 1932) in his book *Markets and Hierarchies* (1975) built on the work of Coase by conceiving of markets and hierarchies as alternative mechanisms for coordinating economic transactions. In his studies on economic development, the economic historian Douglass North (b. 1920) concentrated on the role of institutional change and was one of the pioneers of "cliometrics," theory-based research applying quantitative methods in economic history.

FINANCIAL MARKET THEORY For a long time, work in this area adopted the efficient markets hypothesis, especially as advocated by the Chicago economist Eugene Fama (b. 1939). According to this hypothesis, financial markets ensure that the price of a security contains all relevant information about it at any given time. Financial markets, accordingly, do not leave any room either for systematic error or for the predictive powers of experts. Skepticism as to the validity of this hypothesis could only be amplified by the experience of recurrent bubbles in financial markets and the financial crises that followed their bursting.

However, even the origins of the field nourished skepticism in this regard. The French mathematician Louis Bachelier (1870–1946), with a PhD thesis about speculation published in 1900, is seen as the founder of financial market theory. Bachelier assumed that mistakes made by investors offset each other according to a probability distribution known as Gauss's law, which is represented by the famous "bell curve." Hence, while in the extreme each single actor on the stock exchange may be wrong, in the aggregate they are always right: the market as a whole cannot err.

One of the examiners of Bachelier was Jules Henri Poincaré (1854–1912), the famous French mathematician and philosopher of science. Poincaré put forward two objections against this explanation for the price trend of stocks and the efficiency of financial markets. First, he stressed that one needs to distinguish between systematic and accidental errors. The former obviously do not obey Gauss's law; indeed, they contradict it. The law can therefore apply only to accidental errors. But why should the distribution of accidental errors obey any law—and if it does, why this one? Second, Poincaré insisted that Bachelier had overlooked the all-important fact that man is a gregarious animal, showing herd behavior. Under certain circumstances we follow others, and even if each of these others makes individually only a tiny error, what matters is the accumulation of the same error by many people. This herd behavior involves a systematic failure and disallows any application of Gauss's law in financial market theory. For an insightful study of the complexities involved and the tension between individual and collective rationality, see the book by Alan Kirman (b. 1939) published in 2011. Had Poincaré's insights been absorbed into financial market theory, mankind could perhaps have spared itself some highly unpleasant experiences.

A FINAL WORD

Is the history of economic thought a history of the "wrong ideas of dead men," as Pigou said? Certainly it is partly that, but not only. Knowing the history of the discipline should help us resist superstition, hysteria, and exuberance in economic and social questions. And it should immunize us against the naïve idea that it is the privilege of living economists to articulate only correct ideas.

REFERENCES
AND BIBLIOGRAPHY

(See also the remarks about the literature cited in the concluding paragraph of the introduction.)

Aquinas, Thomas. 2006. *Summa theologiae*, ed. Thomas Gilby. 61 vols. Cambridge: Cambridge University Press. Paperback edition.

Aristotle. 1984. *The Complete Works of Aristotle. The Revised Oxford Translation*. Ed. Jonathan Barnes. 2 vols. Princeton: Princeton University Press.

Arrow, Kenneth J. 1951. *Social Choice and Individual Values*. 2d ed. New York: Wiley, 1963.

——. 1985. *Collected Economic Papers of Kenneth J. Arrow*. 6 vols. Cambridge, MA: Harvard University Press.

Arrow, Kenneth J., and Frank Hahn. 1983. *General Competitive Analysis*. Amsterdam: North Holland.

Atkinson, Anthony B. 2015. *Inequality: What Can Be Done?* Cambridge, MA: Harvard University Press.

St. Augustine of Hippo. 2008. *Confessions*. Ed. Henry Chadwick. Oxford: Oxford University Press.

Béraud, Alain, and Gilbert Faccarello, eds. 2000. *Nouvelle histoire de la pensée économique*. 3 vols. Paris: La Découverte.

Bernoulli, Daniel. 1738. "Specimen theoriae novae de mensura sortis." *Commentarii Academiae Scientiarium Imperalis Petropolitanae*, V: 175–92. English translation as "Exposition of a New Theory on the Measurement of Risk." *Econometrica* 22:23–36.

Blaug, Mark. 1997. *Economic Theory in Retrospect.* 5th ed. Cambridge: Cambridge University Press.

Böhm-Bawerk, Eugen von. 1884–1889. *Kapital und Kapitalzins.* Jena: Fischer. Translated into English as *Capital and Interest.* South Holland, Ill.: Libertarian, 1959.

Buchanan, James M., and Gordon Tullock. 1962. *The Calculus of Consent.* Ann Arbor: University of Michigan Press.

Chamberlin, Edward H. 1933. *The Theory of Monopolistic Competition.* 6th ed. Cambridge, MA: Harvard University Press, 1948.

Chipman, John S. 2013. *German Utility Theory: Analysis and Translations.* Abingdon, UK: Routledge.

Condorcet, Marquis de. 1785. *Essai sur l'application de l'analyse à la probabilité des decisions rendue à la pluralité des voix.* Paris.

Cournot, Antoine Augustin. 1838. *Recherches sur les principes mathématique de la théorie des richesses.* Paris: M. Rivière & Cie. Translated as *Researches into the Mathematical Principles of the Theory of Wealth.* New York: A. M. Kelly, 1960.

Debreu, Gérard. 1959. *Theory of Value.* New York: Wiley.

Domar, Evsey D. 1946. "Capital Expansion, Rate of Growth, and Employment." *Econometrica* 14:137–47.

Dome, Takuo. 1994. *History of Economic Theory. A Critical Introduction.* Aldershot, UK: Edward Elgar.

Edgeworth, Francis Ysidro. 1877. *New and Old Methods of Ethics.* Oxford: James Parker.

——. 1881. *Mathematical Psychics.* London: Kegan Paul.

Ekelund, Robert B., and Robert F. Hébert. 1997. *A History of Economic Theory and Method.* 4th ed. New York: McGraw-Hill.

El-Ashker, A., and R. Wilson. 2006. *Islamic Economics. A Short History.* Boston: Brill Academic.

Faccarello, Gilbert, and Heinz D. Kurz, eds. 2016. *Handbook of the History of Economic Analysis.* 3 vols. Cheltenham: Elgar (forthcoming).

Fisher, Irving. 1906. *The Nature of Capital and Income.* New York: Macmillan.

——. 1907. *The Rate of Interest.* New York: Macmillan.

Foley, Duncan K. 1986. *Understanding Capital: Marx's Economic Theory.* Cambridge, MA: Harvard University Press.

Friedman, Milton. 1969. *The Optimum Quantity of Money, and Other Essays.* Chicago: Aldine.

Garegnani, Pierangelo. 1970. "Heterogeneous Capital, the Production Function and the Theory of Income Distribution." *Review of Economic Studies* 37:407–36.

Gossen, Hermann Heinrich. 1854. *Entwickelung der Gesetze des menschlichen Verkehrs und der daraus fliessenden Regeln für menschliches Handeln.* Braunschweig: Friedrich Vieweg & Sohn. Translated into English as *The Laws of Human Relations and the Rules of Human Action Derived Therefrom*, with an introduction by Nicholas Georgescu-Roegen. Cambridge: MIT Press, 1983.

Harcourt, Geoffrey C. 1972. *Some Cambridge Controversies in the Theory of Capital.* Cambridge: Cambridge University Press.

Harrod, Roy F. 1948. *Towards a Dynamic Economics.* London: Macmillan.

Hayek, F. A. von. 1931. *Prices and Production.* London: Routledge and Kegan Paul.

——. 1945. "The Use of Knowledge in Society." *American Economic Review* 35:519–30.

Hayek, F. A. von, ed. 1935. *Collectivist Economic Planning.* London: Routledge.

Heilbroner, Robert L. 1999. *The Worldly Philosophers.* 7th ed. New York: Simon & Schuster.

Hicks, John R. 1932. *The Theory of Wages.* London: Macmillan.

——. 1937. "Mr. Keynes and the 'Classics': A Suggested Interpretation." *Econometrica* 5:147–59.

——. 1939. *Value and Capital.* 2d ed. Oxford: Oxford University Press, 1946.

——. 1950. *A Contribution to the Theory of the Trade Cycle.* Oxford: Oxford University Press.

Hilferding, Rudolf. 1910. *Das Finanzkapital.* Wien: Ignaz Brand. Translated into English as *Finance Capital.* London: Routledge and Kegan Paul, 1981.

Hotelling, Harold. 1929. "Stability in Competition." *Economic Journal* 39:41–57.

Hu Jichuang. 2009. *A Concise History of Chinese Economic Thought.* Beijing: Foreign Language Teaching and Research Press.

Hume, David. 1985. *Essays: Moral, Political, Literary.* Ed. Eugene F. Miller. Indianapolis: Liberty Classics.

Jevons, William Stanley. 1871. *The Theory of Political Economy.* London: Macmillan. Pelican Classics Edition. Ed. R. D. Collison Black. Harmondsworth, UK: Penguin, 1970.

Kahneman, Daniel, and Amos Tversky, eds. 2000. *Choices, Values, and Frames.* New York: Cambridge University Press.

Kaldor, Nicholas 1978. *Collected Economic Essays.* 6 vols. London: Duckworth.

Kalecki, Michal. 1939. *Essays in the Theory of Economic Fluctuations.* London: Allen & Unwin.

Keynes, John Maynard. 1971–1989. *The Collected Writings of John Maynard Keynes.* Ed. Elizabeth Johnson and Donald Moggridge. 30 vols. London: Macmillan.

Kirman, Alan. 2011. *Complex Economics: Individual and Collective Rationality.* London: Routledge.

Kurz, Heinz D. 2013. *Geschichte des ökonomischen Denkens*. Munich: Beck.

———. 2015a. "Adam Smith on Markets, Competition and Violations of Natural Liberty." *Cambridge Journal of Economics*. doi:10.1093/cje/bev011

———. 2015b. "David Ricardo: On the Art of 'Elucidating Economic Principles' in the Face of a 'Labyrinth of Difficulties.'" *European Journal of the History of Economic Thought*. dx.doi.org/10.1080/09672567.1074713

Kurz, Heinz D., ed. 2008, 2009. *Klassiker des ökonomischen Denkens*. 2 vols. Munich: Beck.

Kurz, Heinz D., and Neri Salvadori. 1995. *Theory of Production. A Long-Period Analysis*. Cambridge: Cambridge University Press.

Lange, Oskar, and Fred M. Taylor. 1938. *On the Economic Theory of Socialism*. New York: McGraw-Hill, 1964.

Leijonhufvud, Axel. 1968. *On Keynesian Economics and the Economics of Keynes*. New York: Oxford University Press.

Leontief, Wassily W. 1941. *The Structure of the American Economy 1919–1939*. New York: Oxford University Press.

Malthus, Thomas R. 1798. *An Essay on the Principle of Population*. London: J. Johnson. Pelican Classics Edition. Ed. Anthony Flew. Harmondsworth, UK: Penguin, 1970.

Marshall, Alfred. 1890. *Principles of Economics*. 8th ed. Variorum Edition. Vols. 1 and 2, 1961. London: Macmillan.

———. 1919. *Industry and Trade*. London: Macmillan.

Marx, Karl. 1867, 1885, 1894. *Das Kapital*. 3 vols. Hamburg: Meissner. Translated into English as *Capital*. Moscow: Progress, vol. 1: 1954; vol. 2: 1956; vol. 3: 1959.

———. 1905–1910. *Theorien über den Mehrwert*, ed. Karl Kautsky. Translated into English as *Theories of Surplus Value*. Moscow: Foreign Language Press, 1963.

Mazzoleni, R. and Richard N. Nelson. 2013. "An Interpretive History of Challenges to Neoclassical Microeconomics and How They Have Fared." *Industrial and Corporate Change* 22:1409–51.

Menger, Carl. 1871. *Grundsätze der Volkswirthschaftslehre*. Wien: Braumüller. Translated into English as *Principles of Economics*. Glencoe, Ill.: Free Press, 1950.

Metcalfe, Stanley. 1998. *Evolutionary Economics and Creative Destruction*. London: Routledge.

Mill, John Stuart. 1967. *Collected Works of John Stuart Mill*. 33 vols. Toronto: University of Toronto Press.

Mises, Ludwig von. 1920. "Die Wirtschaftsrechnung im sozialistischen Gemeinwesen." *Archiv für Sozialwissenschaft und Sozialpolitik* 47:86–121. Translated into English as "Economic Calculation in the Socialist Commonwealth." In *Collectivist Economic Planning*, ed. F. A. Hayek. London: Routledge, 1935.

Mitchell, Wesley C. 1913. *Business Cycles and Their Causes*. California University Memoirs, vol. 3. Berkeley: University of California Press.

Mun, Thomas. 2013. *The Complete Works: Economics and Trade*. n.p.: Newton Page.

Musgrave, Richard A. 1959. *The Theory of Public Finance*. New York: McGraw-Hill.

Myrdal, Gunnar. 1957. *Economic Theory and Underdeveloped Regions*. London: University Paperbacks (Methuen).

Negishi, Takashi. 1989. *History of Economic Theory*. Amsterdam: North-Holland.

Nelson, Richard, and Sidney Winter. 1982. *An Evolutionary Theory of Economic Change*. Cambridge, Mass.: Belknap.

Neumann, John von, and Oskar Morgenstern. 1944. *The Theory of Games and Economic Behavior*. 60th anniv. ed. Princeton, N.J.: Princeton University Press, 2004.

Ohlin, Bertil. 1933. *Interregional and International Trade*. Cambridge, MA: Harvard University Press.

Opocher, Arrigo, and Ian Steedman. 2015. *Full Industry Equilibrium*. Cambridge: Cambridge University Press.

Pareto, Vilfredo. 1971. *Manual of Political Economy*. London: Macmillan.

Patinkin, Don. 1956. *Money, Interest, and Prices. An Integration of Monetary and Value Theory*. 2d (cf. others) ed. New York: Harper & Row.

Phillips, A. William (1958). "The Relationship between Unemployment and the Rate of Change of Money Wages in the United Kingdom 1861–1957." *Economica* 25 (100): 283–99.

Pigou, Arthur C. [1920] 1952. *The Economics of Welfare*. 4th ed. London: Macmillan.

——. [1928] 1947. *A Study in Public Finance*. 3d ed. London: Macmillan.

Piketty, Thomas. 2014. *Capital in the Twenty-First Century*. Cambridge: Harvard University Press.

Plato. 1994. *Republic*. Trans. and with notes and an introduction by Robin Waterfield. Oxford: Oxford World's Classics.

Quesnay, François. 1759. *Tableau économique*. Translated into English as *Quesnay's Tableau Economique* (in parallel with the French text). Trans. Marguerite Kuczynski and Ronald L. Meek. London: Macmillan, 1972.

Ricardo, David. 1951–1973. *The Works and Correspondence of David Ricardo*. Ed. Piero Sraffa with the collaboration of Maurice H. Dobb. 11 vols. Cambridge: Cambridge University Press.

Robbins, Lionel. 1932. *An Essay on the Nature and Significance of Economic Science*. London: Macmillan.

Robinson, Joan. 1933. *The Economics of Imperfect Competition*. 2d ed. London: Macmillan, 1969.

Roncaglia, Alessandro. 2005. *The Wealth of Ideas. A History of Economic Thought*. Cambridge: Cambridge University Press.

Samuels, Warren, Jeff E. Biddle, and John B. Davis, eds. 2003. *A Companion to the History of Economic Thought*. Oxford: Wiley-Blackwell.

Samuelson, Paul A. 1947. *Foundations of Economic Analysis*. Cambridge: Harvard University Press.

——. 1948. *Economics: An Introductory Analysis*. New York: McGraw-Hill.

——. 1966–2011. *Collected Scientific Papers*. Cambridge: MIT Press.

Sandelin, Bo, Hans-Michael Trautwein, and Richard Wundrak. 2015. *A Short History of Economic Thought*. 3d ed. London: Routledge.

Sandmo, Agnar. 2011. *Economics Evolving: A History of Economic Thought*. Princeton, N.J.: Princeton University Press.

Say, Jean-Baptiste. 1803. *Traité d'économie politique*. Translated into English as *A Treatise on Political Economy*. New York: Kelley, 1971.

Schumpeter, Joseph A. 1912. *Theorie der wirtschaftlichen Entwicklung*. Leipzig: Duncker & Humblot. Abridged version translated into English as *The Theory of Economic Development*. Cambridge: Harvard University Press, 1934.

——. "Epochen der Dogmen- und Methodengeschichte." In M. Weber, Ed. *Grundriss der Sozialökonomik*. Part 1. Tübingen: J.C.B. Mohr, 19–124.

——. 1939. *Business Cycles: A Theoretical, Historical, and Statistical Analysis of the Capitalist Process*. 2 vols. New York: McGraw-Hill.

——. 1942. *Capitalism, Socialism, and Democracy*. New York: Harper.

——. 1954. *History of Economic Analysis*. London: Allen & Unwin.

Screpanti, Ernesto, and Stefano Zamagni. 2005. *An Outline of the History of Economic Thought*. Oxford: Oxford University Press.

Sen, Amartya K. 1970. *Collective Choice and Social Welfare*, San Francisco: Holden-Day.

——. 1982. *Poverty and Famines: An Essay on Entitlement and Deprivation*. Oxford: Clarendon Press.

——. 2010. *The Idea of Justice*. London: Penguin.

Smith, Adam. 1759. *The Theory of Moral Sentiments*. London: Millar. Glasgow Bicentenary Edition. Ed. D. D. Raphael and A. L. Macfie. Oxford: Oxford University Press, 1976.

——. 1776. *An Inquiry Into the Nature and Causes of the Wealth of Nations*. London: Strahan and Cadell. Glasgow Bicentenary Edition. Ed. R.H. Campbell and A.S. Skinner. Oxford: Oxford University Press, 1976.

Solow, Robert M. 1956. "A Contribution to the Theory of Economic Growth." *Quarterly Journal of Economics* 70:65–94.

Spiegel, Henry William. 1991. *The Growth of Economic Thought.* 3d ed. Durham, N.C.: Duke University Press.

Sraffa, Piero. 1925. "Sulle relazioni fra costo e quantità prodotta." *Annali di economia* 2:277–328. Translated into English. In *Italian Economic Papers*, ed. Luigi L. Pasinetti, 323–63. Bologna: Il Mulino, 1998. Reprinted in H. D. Kurz and N. Salvadori, eds. 2003. *The Legacy of Sraffa.* Vol. 1. Cheltenham, UK: Elgar, 3–43.

——. 1926. "The Laws of Returns Under Competitive Conditions." *Economic Journal* 36:535–50.

——. 1960. *Production of Commodities by Means of Commodities.* Cambridge: Cambridge University Press.

Steedman, Ian. 1977. *Marx after Sraffa.* London: New Left Books.

Stiglitz, Joseph E. 1969. "The Effects of Income, Wealth and Capital Gains Taxation on Risk-Taking." *Quarterly Journal of Economics* 83:262–83.

——. 1994. *Whither Socialism?* Cambridge: MIT Press.

Sweezy, Paul M. 1942. *The Theory of Capitalist Development.* New York: Oxford University Press.

Thünen, Johann Heinrich von. 1826, 1850. *Der isolierte Staat in Beziehung auf Landwirthschaft und Nationalökonomie.* Vols. 1 and 2. Translated in part into English as *Von Thünen's Isolated State.* Ed. Peter Hall. Oxford: Pergamon, 1966.

Tsoulfidis, Lefteris. 2009. *Competing Schools of Economic Thought.* Heidelberg: Springer.

Veblen, Thorstein. 1899. *The Theory of the Leisure Class.* New York: Macmillan.

——. 1904. *The Theory of Business Enterprise.* New York: Scribner.

Walras, Léon. 1874, 1877. *Éléments d'économie politique pure.* Lausanne: Corbaz. Translated into English as *Elements of Pure Economics.* Trans. and with an introduction by William Jaffé. Homewood, Ill.: Irwin, 1954.

Wicksell, Knut. 1893. *Über Wert, Kapital und Rente.* Translated into English as *Value, Capital, and Rent.* London: Allen & Unwin, 1954.

——. 1898. *Geldzins und Güterpreise.* Jena: Fischer. Translated into English as *Interest and Prices.* London: Macmillan, 1936.

Wieser, Friedrich von. 1889. *Der natürliche Wert.* Wien: Hölder. Translated into English as *Natural Value.* New York: Kelley & Millman, 1956.

INDEX

Page numbers in italics indicate figures or tables.